EXPLORING FICTIONAL WORLD OF WILLIAM GOLDING

EXPLORING FICTIONAL WORLD OF WILLIAM GOLDING

Juthika Bhattacharjee

AKANSHA PUBLISHING HOUSE
NEW DELHI • GUWAHATI • VISAKHAPATNAM

AKANSHA PUBLISHING HOUSE
4649-B/21, Ansari Road
Darya Ganj, New Delhi - 110 002
Ph.: 23263193 / 9811582579 / 09435116718
Fax: 011-23263193
Email: ektabooks@yahoo.com
www.akanshapublishinghouse.com

Exploring Fictional World of William Golding

First Published 2011
ISBN 978-81-8370-282-9

PRINTED IN INDIA

Published by Akansha Publishing House, New Delhi and Printed at Harmain Offset Press, Delhi.

Contents

Preface

William Goding (1911 -1993) is a distinguished figure in contemporary British fiction. He was awarded the Nobel Prize for literature in 1983. Of his twelve novels, those written before 1965 have drawn due attention from critics. His first novel *Lord of the Flies* and the subsequent novels, published till 1964, have received wide critical attention. Some of the important works to be cited in this respect are: Mark Kinkead-Weekes and Ian Gregor, William Golding, A Critical Study (1967) ; Virginia Tiger, William Golding, The Dark Fields of Discovery (1976); Howard S. Babb, The Novels of William Golding (1970) ; Bernard F. Dick William Golding (1967); and Oldsey and Weintraub The Art of William Golding (1965). But there is still much scope for a detailed critical reading of his later novels, particularly those written after The Spire (1964). The present work proposes to do this. Its aim is, precisely, to attempt a critical evaluation of the later novels of Golding, seven in all, with regard to their matter and form. They are *The Pyramid* (1967), *The Scorpion God* (1971), *Darkness Visible* (1979), *Rites of Passage* (1980), *The Paper Men* (1984), *Close Quarters* (1987), and *Fire Down Below* (1989). These novels, however, cannot be evaluated in total isolation from Golding's earlier ones. As such it was considered necessary to give an idea of his early novels in the first chapter of this work where an overview of the fictional world of William Golding has been presented to facilitate the discussion of the later novels in the chapters that follow. In the present study they have been related to the earlier ones, as and when necessary, thus enabling us to see the continuity of Golding's career as a novelist, and his unified perspective on life and things. His works, when examined in their totality, reveal a gradual change in his world view from one of grief and gloom to one of light and hope.

It has been our endeavour here to examine the theme of each novel under separate chapters. The form of every one of the novels has been examined towards the close of each chapter.

In this study we have concentrated on a close reading of the texts and a threadbare analysis of their themes and characters and techniques, for a proper assessment of Golding's achievement. Our approach, thus, has been mainly textual and analytical.

Juthika Bhattacharjee

Acknowledgements

I record my profound gratitude to Prof. P. Kotoky for introducing me to the world of William Golding and his help in completing this work.

I am happy to acknowledge my gratitude to the Assistant Librarians of National Library, Calcutta, who have helped whole–heartedly in a number of ways, and also to the British Council Library, Calcutta, K.K. Handique Library, Gauhati University and NEHU Library, Shillong.

I owe my thanks to Rev. Thomas Pullipurambil and to Mr. Ananya Shankar Guha, both of whom helped by providing some valuable critical works on Golding.

I express my deep gratitude to my husband Mr. B. Bhattacharjee and my son Dipayan Bhattacharjee who have been lovingly patient during the making of this work. With their readiness to forego a number of pleasures for the sake of this work, they have been the essential source of my energy.

Finally, I am thankful to Mr. M.P. Misra, Akansha Publishing House, New Delhi for undertaking publication of this work.

Juthika Bhattacharjee

1

The World of William Golding's Fiction

William Gerald Golding (1911 – 1993) has come to occupy an important position in the pantheon of modern British fiction. An ex-schoolmaster, an eminent classical scholar, anthropologist, actor, Egyptophile, musician, a Royal Navy lieutenant in command of a rocket ship during the World War II, possessor of an intellect of towering proportions, Golding arrests the imagination of the reader with immediacy and certainty. Using the allegory to portray man's constant struggle between the civilized self and darker side of his nature, Golding has earned himself the reputation of having done more for the modern British novel than any other of the novelists of his time. Writing with the sensitivity of a poet, he has been hailed by some as a modern Conrad. Seeing things from a perspective that is personal, corrective, and highly original, he has treated different subjects in different novels, putting them at different times and places. The manner of treatment varies from novel to novel. Yet he has worked within the pale of recognizable forms. Thanks to his broad religious outlook, his work has gained wide popularity outside England also.

Born into an English middle-class academic family, Golding had a childhood which was rather idyllic and isolated. After graduating from Oxford, he spent some time in a theatre, and later became a schoolmaster at Bishop Wordsworth's school. With the outbreak of the war, he joined the Royal Navy and was in active service for almost the entire period the war lasted. The war, awakening both the man and the writer in him, had an important influence. The World War II was a turning point in his life as he began to see what people were capable of doing. Through his fiction he has attempted to preserve sanity and morality in a world torn by two wars and tried to construct a religious mythopoeia relevant to contemporary man'. [1]

Golding has shown his concern for problems and issues similar to those of several of his contemporaries like Graham Greene, Angus Wilson, and Iris Murdoch. Golding and Greene bear a similarity in the sense that they both look at the fundamental human situation in a contemporary setting. What Walter Allen has observed of Greene is largely true of Golding too. He says

> From the beginning he has been obsessed with the plight of fallen man, with the split in man's mind, the insidious attraction of evil, the insidious attraction of good; and he has always been obsessed by the meaninglessness, the seediness . . ., the vulgarity of a world he describes is very largely the world of rootless, beliefless urban man, and he describes it with compelling vividness and in terms of a fascinated loathing in which there is always an element of love entwined with hate. He contemplates it and renders it with horror and with pity. As a Christian, he sees his characters . . . under the aspect of eternity. ...[2]

Golding's preoccupation with evil shows some closeness of approach with that of Angus Wilson on the same subject. It is relevant to quote here the latter's observations as revealed in an article called 'Evil in the English Novel'. It reads:

> I have been led to suppose that one of the troubles is that we are too much concerned with right and wrong, and not enough with evil. As an agnostic writer

> with apprehensions of evil over and above my ideas of right and wrong, I have been concerned to try to find ways of introducing evil into my novels.[3]

William Golding's concern, too, has been to diagnose the ills of human nature, to look at what is permanent in man and to study him in relation to his cosmic situation. In his essay 'Belief and Creativity' he says:

> What man is whatever man is under the eye of heaven, that I burn to know and that – I do not say this lightly– I would endure knowing. The themes closest to my purpose, to my imagination have stemmed from that preoccupation, have been of such a sort that they might move me a little nearer that knowledge. They have been themes of man at an extremity, man tested like building material, taken into the laboratory and used to destruction; man isolated, man obsessed, man drowning in a literal sea or in the sea of his own ignorance.[4]

In his fiction Golding has tried to communicate a vision of reality. He believes that evil, in the form of darkness, emanates from man himself. Darkness, which inhabits the core of man's being, by controlling his character, becomes the central organizing principle. Taking the form of egoism it leads on to hatred, pride, immorality, and atheism which, in their turn, bring nothing but ruin to the individual. Darkness has led modern man farther and farther away from the root of his being. An isolated creature's sense of his innermost self is Golding's metaphor for depicting this spiritual experience – man's cognizance of his innermost self in front of a pig's head or struggling for survival in the sea or confronting his self in a dark prison cell or before a dark pit. Golding insists that this kind of experience is essential for a realization of the Divine. But it is left to the men who suffer for the sake of other men, the saints in the society, to embrace darkness, discover its essence, and purge this world of evil. To the ignorant, the saint becomes a proof of the existence of God.

Being pre-eminently concerned with the power of darkness, Golding's fiction depicts characters who turn away from God and create their own world out of evil. This evil or darkness, which inhabits the centre of a being, though elusive, is constantly watchful. As one of his characters puts it:

> It is the unnameable, unfathomable and invisible darkness that sits at the centre of him, always awake, always different from what you believe it to be, always thinking and feeling what you can never know it thinks and feels, that hopes hopelessly to understand and to be understood. Our loneliness is the loneliness not of the cell or the castaway; it is the loneliness of that dark thing.[5]

Modern man's capacity for evil stems from his extreme selfishness and insufficiently evolved consciousness. This egoism, which is the root of violence and wickedness, if not disciplined in time, will bring further destruction. In an interview Golding stated:

> I think [selfishness is] a question of self-awareness . . . Now with our awareness of ourselves as individuals inescapably comes in this other thing, this destructive thing, the evil, if you like. It seems to me that this self- awareness, intelligence, with these come the defect of their virtue. We have to learn, and it's quite possible, I think, that we never shall learn, that is a species that will be the thing which will trip us up, our own intelligence and our own lusts. But if we are going to survive those two aspects of man, his selfishness and his intelligence, we've got to learn to control those,otherwise they tend to destroy us, I think they are what mark us off from the animal kingdom, so far as we are marked off from it.[6]

Evil is inherent in man's soul ready to put forth its strength whenever the occasion is favourable for it. In *Lord of the Flies* a group of school children on an island are propelled by it to a condition of animality. They torture and murder, converting the island into a veritable hell with their ritualistic chants 'Kill the Beast! Cut his throat!' Evil, though externalized as 'The Beast', has a human face. Simon, who understands that evil is 'only us' becomes the victim of violent murderous force. The noble, unselfish, emotional, and spiritual Simons, who lay down their lives for humanity, remain beyond the pale of comprehension of the common man.

Though man is sinful by nature, Golding insists that he must learn to live without greed. In an interview with James Baker he said:

> I remember alluding in passing to the idea of original sin and I suppose allowing it to be inferred that I believe in original sin and somebody else there, a scientist, really got rather angry ... he said all this talk about original sin is absolutely nonsense, that man is a creature who suffers from an innate inability to live a proper and satisfactory life in a social circumstance. And I said, well, that's an elaborate definition of original sin and I cannot, I have never been able to see how anybody can deny what stares us in the face— unless we control ourselves, we sin. Our nature is to want to grab some- thing that belongs to somebody else, and we have either to be taught or teach ourselves that you've got to share, you can't grab the lot. And for God's sake, history is really no more than a chronicle of original sin.[7]

Human nature, clinging to egoism and combative animality, gives rise to sin which is not a cosmic accident. Even animals fail to be as viciously cruel, dangerously violent, and persistently wicked as man has shown himself capable of in the last few wars. His selfishness, wedded to his intellectual cunning, has wrought widespread havoc. In *The Inheritors* the new men triumph over the innocent Neanderthals with their ability to be cruel. Their superior intelligence, being a result of their knowledge of evil, is instrumental in exterminating the Neanderthals. Their world, contrasted with that of the Neanderthals who are simple and incapable of understanding the killing instincts of the new men, is depraved with child murder, violence and lustful orgies, superstition, wickedness, sadism and callousness. *The Inheritors,* reflecting a reversal of Wellsian optimism regarding man, reveals man's 'appalling ignorance of his own nature'.

In *Pincher Martin* the effort of a dead man's monstrous ego to remain intact by inventing a rock in the Atlantic are presented through an ingenious narrative device whereby metaphysical concepts are given in the shape of physical realities. Pincher Martin refuses to acknowledge the cosmic chaos of death by clinging, with fierce desperation, to his existence. The fantasy existence permits him to retain his personal identity in the face of his terror of the infinite. Christopher Martin represents modern man and Golding's explanation of the character is illuminating:

> Christopher Hadly Martin had no belief in anything but the importance of his own life, no God. Because he was created in the image of God he had a freedom of choice which he used to centre the world on himself. He did not believe in purgatory and therefore when he died it was not presented to him in overtly theological terms. The greed of life which had been the mainspring of his nature forced him to refuse the selfless act of dying. He continued to exist separately in a world composed of his own murderous nature. His drowned body lies rolling in the Atlantic but the ravenous ego invents a rock for him to endure on. It is the memory of an aching tooth. Ostensibly and rationally he is a survivor from a torpedoed destroyer: but deep down he knows the truth. He is not fighting for bodily survival but for his continuing identity in face of what will smash it and sweep it away — the black lightning, the compassion of God. For Christopher, the Christ-bearer has become Pincher Martin who is little but greed. Just to be Pincher is purgatory: to be Pincher for eternity is hell.[8]

Pincher Martin, an intellectual and an atheist, is a rational empiricist whose selfish view blurs reality. Choosing greed instead of grace of God, he reveals himself as an adulterer, a homosexual, a thief, a rapist, and a would-be-murderer. This voluptuousness is expressed through the metaphor of eating:

> The whole business of eating was peculiarly significant. They made a ritual of it on every level, the Fascists as a punishment, the religious as a rite, the cannibal either as a ritual or as a medicine or as a superbly direct declaration to conquest. Killed and eaten. And of course eating with the mouth was only the gross expression of what was a universal process. You could eat with hobnailed boots or buying and selling or marrying and begetting cuckolding...(88).

He represents the twentieth-century man's self-centred perspective of the world which makes him aggressive and dangerous causing limitless suffering and misery.

Pincher's egoism and pride prevent him from recognizing the all-powerful and all-compassionate God appearing as 'black lightning'. Owing to excessive greed and conceit, a self-incurred destiny becomes preferable to submitting oneself to the cosmic vitality. Usurping the role of the creator, he makes a world and time out of the formless void and darkness. God is created in his own image. This self-created nightmare, the result of extreme egotism, becomes the cause of psychic suffering pushing him into further unbalance. Relief comes in the form of 'black lighting', the compassion of God. Modern man's intellect, rationalism, and arrogant pride have made him indifferent to the experience of the numinous increasing enormously his own agony and despair.

Contemporary man's egotistical clinging to the materialistic life has put him in a state of free fall whereby he has lost contact with faith, goodness, love, sympathy, compassion, and tenderness. Sammy's spiritual crisis is representative of modern man's crisis caused by his loss of faith and belief. Golding explains:

> Without a system of values, without an adherence to some, one might almost call it, codified morality, right and wrong, you are like a creature in space, tumbling, eternally tumbling, no up, no down, just in 'free fall' in the scientific sense. Also, of course, you can link it with the Miltonic idea, sufficient to have stood though free to fall; and link it, therefore, with the Miltonic concept of free will. Those two things were in my mind, but mostly the scientific one, because it's a convenient metaphor in a way, that the more science you get the more it is easy for old systems to be struck away, old supports to be knocked down and for people to find themselves in a state of free fall, just as science and technology can get you to the position where you can actually put a man in to free fall... I've found the metaphor adequate for my purpose, but of course also there is inherent, should be inherent in the book... the fact that man is, I believe, by nature a moral creature, and when he's in free fall he, so to speak, stumbles over his morals without knowing they are there. He exploits people and then finds that with this comes guilt and that you can't be free of right and wrong because you know by some kind of instinct when you've exploited somebody, when you've hurt somebody, when you have cheated somebody. You know when you lie and all the rest of it. It's no good saying none of these things matter. They do. They matter intensely to man because he is not just man, he is a social being.[9]

Contrasted with the defined areas of conflict of the earlier books, *Free Fall* evinces a slight change in Golding's view of the cosmos and the human condition opening a way to the mysteries, doubts, despair, and hopes of the later works. As Peter Green has pointed out,

> Sammy speaks for himself, and therefore, inevitably, with a degree of self - justification as well as guilty

> self - reproach. He is asking questions, not imposing patterns ; shaking the bars of his cage, challenging his own inner convictions. Sammy, the contemporary, fumbling , destructive , yet essentially well meaning hedonist . . . Sammy the visionary , the artist , who loves his coarse Welsh wife with a ferocious tenderness, however he may ruin the Beatrices of this world - Sammy is the character through whom Mr. Golding, one suspects, is beginning to be reconciled to the loss of the primal Eden. [10]

Having glimpsed the reality of the moral world, Sammy understands the need for a morality in individual relationships, and accepts the burden of his guilt. Knowing the impossibility of ever again living contentedly with his own nature, Sammy recognizes 'cosmic chaos' as the basic condition of human existence.

The Spire concentrates attention on the solution of spiritual and aesthetic dilemmas and, at the same time, examines man's vulnerability, and his involvement with evil while he is aspiring towards the divine and the aesthetic. Though both light and darkness press upon him, man's conscious volition for egotism has made him incapable of defeating the dark forces in him.

Selfishness, the off shoot of the dark half of human nature, tends to suppress qualities like love, sympathy, compassion, and forgiveness. It gives rise to hatred, pride, and immorality. How a lack of love can degrade people in society is demonstrated in *The Pyramid.* In this novel (and later in the trilogy of *Rites of Passage),* Golding expresses his strong disapproval of the class system which is depicted effectively through English provincial life and its rigid class structure. Breeding exploitation, hatred, and snobbery , it has become a source of darkness in society. Henry, in order to ascend the ladder of class, exploits Bounce Dawlish for money and in the process is rendered incapable of genuine love. His failure to respond warmly to Bounce's love pushes her slowly towards the dark pit of insanity. Egotism, on the social level, makes people calculating and unemotional. While Oliver regards Evie as an object to be used for his own sexual satisfaction, Henry humours Bounce for his own materialistic ends. They represent the type of people who are ready to pay only a reasonable price to help others and achieve their ends. Regarding nothing as sacred, selfishness breeds arrogance, terrorism, crime and unimaginable horrors. Self-worship, the cause of the two world wars, the Vietnam war, and the Gulf war, may beget still more horrible atrocities in future. The title, *The Pyramid,* though suggesting an idea of social ascent, is much more effective in implying a spiritual death as a result of a lack of love. Music, the metaphor for love, fails to bring harmony in Stilbourne as depicted by the episode of *The King of Hearts* produced by the Stilbourne Operatic Society. Bounce, rebelling against her father's phrase, 'Heaven is Music', and his lack of sympathy, destroys music books, papers, metronome, and a bust of Beethoven. A dead society is incapable of appreciating music. Consequently, Oliver, whose first love is music, ends up making poison gas. In the rigid class society of Stilbourne (the name is suggestive) the inmates fail in love. As Golding says , 'the class society is a function of the people. People are, in their turn, to some extent, a function of the society, and it is difficult to love'. [11]

It has been Golding's constant effort to bring back the religious dimensions of human experience through the body of his fiction which rouses one from a state of apathy to one of positive interest in the human condition. He endeavours to make us recognize that unless human consciousness undergoes a transformation from egoism to selflessness, survival in this world will be impossible. The failure of the human race to saddle its intelligence, lust, selfishness, and pride will result in its destruction. By projecting his own dark nature on the universe, man tends, inevitably, to vitiate its atmosphere. As Golding says,

> I think it's quite likely that we've Got black holes out there because we have discovered them in here . . . we've done some things in this century that we didn't think human beings could do and which are indescribable, and those are black holes in a way. So the next thing we do is find them out there in the

> universe . . . I think there has been a tendency in man's mind, man's nature, to make the universe in the image of his own mind. After all, there is very little else he can do with it.[12]

Having no confidence in religious institutions, dogmas, or hierarchies, Golding seems to have subscribed to some fundamental articles of the Christian faith. He has expressed his views in an essay:

> Man is a fallen being. He is gripped by original sin. His nature is sinful and his state perilous. I accept the theology and admit the triteness ; but what is trite is true; and a truism can become more than a truism when it is a belief passionately held. [13]

Being convinced of the morally diseased nature of man, Golding seeks to reveal the connection between man's brute nature and the 'chaos of existence'. The endeavour of a group of school boys to construct a civilization in a desert island, is foiled, not by any outside force, but by their own diseased nature. Sammy's own nature compels him to hurt and betray the innocent Beatrice. Pincher's greed, lust, avarice, and pride portray man's basic sickness. Jocelin, Oliver, Barclay, and Sophy are no exceptions. Sadism, cynicism, treachery, disloyalty, and nihilism, portrayed in Sophy, compel man to transgress and destabilize the force of nature. The self-love of Oliver and Barclay, while inducing them to exploit others, forces them to remain insensitive to others' feelings.

Golding believes that man's nature is sinful, and that his being is in danger because he is in the clutches of original sin. But, being created in the image of God, man has free will by which he can turn either away from Him or towards Him. Pincher, by choosing to ignore God, has condemned himself to one of the eternally damned. Sophy's passion for 'weirdness' renders her powerless to glimpse, even for a moment, the beauty and harmony of the creation. But Sammy is fortunate because although he chooses to turn away from God, he has cognizance of the Good, inherent in the dark nature of his being. Jocelin's pride blinds him but illumination comes towards the end. The average man, being ignorant of the spiritual world, tends to stumble over morality. Failing to diagnose the evil from which he suffers, he makes mistakes. For him, only the physical world being coherent, the spiritual is inconsequential. Having only flashes of religious experience, the numinous remains incoherent to him.

While Golding is grieved to glimpse the dark part of human nature, he is occasionally convinced that the world is a veritable hell with the devil stalking it. In *Darkness Visible* though Matty is convinced of the presence of God, Sophy is impelled to do evil by the dark thing she imagines to be sitting at the back of her mind. In *The Paper Men* Barclay, too, is convinced that the world is a hell where man is constantly damning himself. At times the Good and the Evil work hand in hand. Though Colley sees the grace of God reflected in all His creation – the air, the sea, and the sun – he is impelled by the dark part of his nature to have a weakness for the handsome Billy Rogers. The characters live or perish in accordance with the writer's world view. Therefore Simon and Matty perish as a result of man's evil nature.

A genuine religion, which concerns itself with selflessness, is Golding's creed. Advocating simplicity, goodness, and sympathy for fellow beings, Golding has expressed the belief that the world can be held together only by recapturing the biblical traditions. Matty, in his disinterested love for human beings, devotes his life to the service of mankind. He believes whole-heartedly that good can come to this world through the holiness of men if not through the holy spirit. Nathaniel, too, typifies a highly creative force which awakens the inherently spiritual qualities in human beings. These are the qualities which are generally neglected by the average person. Golding endeavours to convince his readers, through characters like Nathaniel and Matty, of the presence of a mystical power which evokes awe, wonder, and reverence. They try to recapture the language of innocence, love, goodness, and kindness. A balance between reason and intuition is imperative for the harmonious development of not only of the human personality but also of society as a whole. In *Lord of the Flies,* as long as Simon's intuitions are balanced against Piggy's reason, there is the semblance of harmony in society. In *Lord of the Flies* with their death, terror and murder break loose on the island. Defying all kinds of rationalism, some of Golding's characters, who can be called mystics, try to resist evil with their power to do good. Simon, who has clarity of vision, knows that evil does not come in the form of any external beast but is ingrained in human nature. For the salvation of his fellow beings it becomes necessary for him to convey this wisdom to them. Nathaniel, who is a compendium of the many good people Golding has known, resembles Simon, for he, too, warns Pincher of a purgatory. Nathaniel represents a force which is instrumental in liberating the inherent spiritual qualities of individuals who are generally ignorant of their capacity for the numinous. Matty is the super- rational being who, with his religious and mystical experience, demonstrates man's capacity for elevating himself to the superhuman. He awakens one to the fact that beyond the physical, which is temporal, there is the mystical for the attainment of which we must devote our energy. In this age of rationalism, science, and technology, man has increasingly turned away from God. For him the physical, and everything related to it, has become all important. Ignoring the fact that he has to discard this body some day, he engrosses himself in egotism. Through saintly characters like Simon, Lok, Nathaniel, Beatrice, Matty, and Colley, Golding seeks to make contemporary man conscious of the presence of a mystical world and the need to turn to it. Fallen beings may torture or ignore them – Simon is brutally murdered; Lok becomes the victim of organized torture; Nathaniel becomes a prey to derision; Beatrice suffers from psycho neuroticism as a result of Sammy's betrayal; Matty is ignored, rejected, and exploited by the people for whom he dedicates his life; Colley is humiliated and meets his death – but saints cannot be stopped from loving their fellow beings with a constancy which springs from an essentially forgiving nature.

Depicting the human condition, the body of Golding's fiction points out that the present world can survive only if it has people like Matty, Simon, Nathaniel or Summers, who are dedicated to the common cause. Golding's belief is that there is a moral order in this world. Once this order is disturbed, there is darkness and cosmic chaos. It is saints like Mattys and Simons who keep up this order at the cost of their lives. Teaching human beings to turn away from the darkness of egotism to God, they stand for the moral order which is an attribute of the spiritual world. Unless a person is wholly given up to evil (like Sophy in *Darkness Visible*) there is hope for his redemption as is evident from the life of Mr. Pedigree who had sinned as a homosexual but was shown the way to salvation by Matty. The beauty and harmony of the spiritual world is evinced by Pedigree towards the end of his life.

The working of one's salvation is demonstrated by Matty who undergoes physical mortification and accepts sacrificial death for the general good. With his intuitive and mystical vision of reality, Matty brings light to a world of evil and·darkness. Simon, Nathaniel, and Summers, too, with their activities, point out that in spite of the evil in this world, there is a good which is ultimate and absolute. Through Matty, Golding convinces the reader of the presence of a divine grace in this world. Men like him guide common man away from a selfish existence to a realization of the supreme will.

Golding, with his deep faith in God, evokes the mystery at the heart of things. In his lecture *Belief and Creativity* he admits of his belief in God. All his novels, with their complexity and ambiguity, bear testimony to his most deeply held conviction. As Ian Gregor has pointed out, 'when we talk of Golding's exercising a religious imagination we feel that the primary effort has been to make us feel, within this world, the overwhelming importance of a world elsewhere, more precisely, a Creator elsewhere.' 14 In a world where scientific rationalism is increasingly making people ridicule the idea of God, Golding positively asserts his faith in the Absolute. He remarks:

> My guess is that there are infinite Cosmoses . . . and beyond that is the thing I call the Good [God]. It seems

> to me that there could be infinite modes of life, and that they would all be sustained by the beings that inhabit them. In other words, we have invented our own universe. We have discovered that there are black holes out there because we have Hiroshima and Belsen in here. We have made black holes in here and then discovered them out there . . . . May be there are universes of awful suffering, may be there are universes of awful pleasure, but I guess that beyond them there must be a Good which is Abso- lute . . . . So when you ask me if I believe in God it's not even a matter of what I believe. It's what I suspect.[15]

Golding convinces us of the urgency of his belief by stressing the importance of leading a kind of life based upon love. His later novels increasingly stress the need of awakening a longing for the spiritual, through love. The epigraph from *The Pyramid* is indicative of the same: 'If thou be among people make for thyself love, the beginning and the end of the heart'. Man alone can improve this world, bringing goodness into it, through his own nature.

Golding's broad humanity, combined with a deep patriotic feeling for England and her people, has prompted him to attack the adherence of the English to the evils of the class system. He says, ' I condemn and detest my country's faults precisely because I am so proud of her many virtues.'[16] *Lord of the Flies* depicts the falsity of the sense of superiority of the English as reflected in Ballantyne's view of the English boys who exhibit a national temper 'which subdues tropical islands as triumphantly as England imposes empire and religion on lawless breeds of men'. Jack and his tribe', who are thoroughly English, behave in a manner which would put any savage to shame. The naval officer's comment, 'I should have thought that a pack of British boys . .', you're all British aren't you? . . would have been able to put up a better show than that . .', brings into relief the murderous activities of the boys . . they had already killed Simon and Piggy and were hunting down Ralph who would have inevitably met the same fate had not the officer intervened. Golding opines that human beings are basically the same everywhere. He points out that 'one lot of people is inherently like any other lot of people; . . . the only enemy of man is inside him'.[17] Abhorrent nationalism often becomes an excuse for savagery and blood lust. British society, along with a few other societies (the case of India may be cited here), is a victim of the vicious class- system. A society in its clutches tends to meet a slow death. Stilbourne in *The Pyramid*, and the ship in *Rites of Passage* and its sequels, depict, in miniature, the British class-system. Golding observes, 'Unless we can get rid of it or at least blunt the Pyramid or make it a little less monumental, we're done, we're finished, and it had better happen quickly' 18. A result of man's dark nature, the class system is the source of wickedness in society.

Golding has used a wide range of scenes and actions in his novels. As regards his characters, however, most of them are English. The action of *Lord of the Flies* takes place in a desert island in the Pacific Ocean but the characters are all English boys. Though the dead airman is Japanese, the Naval Officer, who rescues the boys, is again English. Pincher Martin, in the novel of the same name, drowning in the Atlantic, has memories of his past life spent in his own country, England. The major portion of the action of Free Fall takes place in London and, except for Dr. Halde and the German soldiers, all the characters are English. Jocelin, who has the inspiration to get the spire on a cathedral (resembling the one in Salisbury, England) constructed, is himself English and uses people who are all English. The Pyramid is the most English of all of Golding's novels — the setting, Stilbourne (Marlborough of Golding's youth), the class-conscious village people and their snobbery, all add to the geographical and social reality which is very much English. In *Darkness Visible* the cosmic struggle is depicted through Matty and Sophy who were born and brought up in England. All the three parts of the novel have England as the scene of action except for a portion of Part One, which takes place in Australia where Matty's search for identity gets intensified. The vivid description of twentieth-century London and the English countryside forcefully brings home the morally degraded condition of modern man. Pedigree, Sim Goodchild, and Edwin Bell are English in their ways and manners. *Rites of Passage* with its two sequels resembles *The Pyramid* for portraying the evils of the English class-structure. All the characters in the ship sailing towards Australia are English, while the historical incident, around which the story is built, is of the Regency period. The protagonist of *The Paper Men*, contantly moving from one European country to another, meets his nemesis in England. By birth he is English, though his tormenter, Rick Tucker, is American. Golding, himself an inveterate traveler, admitted his weakness for England in an interview in these words:

> All I can say is that I stay home. Exile may be O. K. for other people, and there have often been times I wanted to live abroad, but then I've gone and seen Englishmen who were exiled and thought; Lord preserve me. So although I do a great deal of traveling, alas less the older I get, I've never pretended to be other than English and to live anywhere but England . . . it's just a fact of my life.[19]

The fact of his being English does not make it obligatory for him to choose only British themes or characters for his fiction. He is an individualist with a cosmopolitan view of the world.

Golding's uniqueness and originality, as a novelist, lies in his capacity to experiment not only with daring themes, but also with unusual forms and techniques. As Mark Kinkead-Weekes and I an Greagor put it very effectively:

> . . . however densely imagined a particular character or episode may be, everything has been pared down, stripped of irrelevant detail. Bringing these impressions together, we might say that a Golding novel gives the effect or something dedicatedly made, every strain and stress calculated and overcome , so that the final product leads us to think in terms of a sculpture.[20]

His novels get form and direction from strong moral assumptions. As the novelist himself observed, 'In all my books, I have suggested a shape in the universe that may, as it were, account for things'. Rigorously organized and heavily controlled, most of his novels are expressions of moral ideas. As Frank Kermode puts it, 'It is a mark of Golding's integrity that in every book he employs technical devices of remarkable ingenuity but never indulges his skill; it is never a hair's breadth in excess of what the moral occasion demands'.[21] Golding avers that guilt is greater in a world which does not punish evil than in one that sequestrates. Leaving out all that is extraneous, the language of his fiction acquires the intensity and spontanaeity of poetry. Choosing themes that isolate what is basic, Golding forces his readers to identify themselves with the moral of the theme rather than with the characters. In the choice of subject-matter and style, Golding has deviated from the contemporary trend. As Karl, F. has rightly commented.,

> In each of the novels, the manner is indirect, the symbols rarely clarified, and the method of narration uncondescending and stringent. Golding is obviously striving to move behind the conventional matter of contemporary novel to a view of what man, or pre – man is really like when his façade of civilized behaviour falls away.[22]

Golding's novels, generally short and densely textured, have a prose which is strenuous, compact, angular, ablique, and elliptical. His characters are usually three dimensional human beings but they often function as expositors of facets of man's nature — Ralph as common sense, Piggy as intellectualism or rationalism, Pincher as greed, Jocelin as pride, Simon, Matty , and Nathaniel as man's goodness, Sophy as evil in man, Barclay as selfishness — without becoming abstractions.

Proclaiming himself frankly a 'fabulist' and a moralist and expressing his concern with what is basic in human nature, Golding lays stress more on the significance of the theme of the novel than on the characters and the situations. He is concerned more with ideas than with characters. Being preoccupied with examining the nature of the universe, the characters in his fiction tend to be closed, and resistant to change. The leading personages being mostly males, Golding looks at women from the outside only. While female characters have been completely excluded from *Lord of the Flies,* there is only a passing reference to some women in *Pincher Martin.* Just as Beatrice of *Free Fall* is the epitome of goodness, Sophy in *Darkness Visible* is the very incarnation of evil, and fails to be a woman of flesh and blood. The female characters of *The Paper Men* and the trilogy consisting of *Rites of Passage, Close Quarters* and *Fire Down Below,* too, have been drawn very sketchily.

Golding's novels create the impression of being at once simple and complicated owing to his complex vision of the world. By juxtaposing paradoxes of existence through the paradoxical structure of each novel, Golding seeks to make the reader comprehend the quality of the spiritual world. Superficially, the story often becomes ambiguous as it is presented through the eyes of a person whose mentality is quite alien to the reader's own — Lok in *The Inheritors,* Pincher in *Pincher Martin,* Dean Jocelin in *The Spire,* Matty in *Darkness Visible,* Barclay in *ThePaper Men.* The Neanderthal man has a thought process which is not thoroughly developed; Pincher Martin, though modern and urban, is egotistical to the extreme; Jocelin is a visionary often appearing to be mad; Matty is unworldly and mystical with unique compassion beyond human comprehension; Barclay is callous and intensely self-absorbed. All the novels, except *Free Fall, The Pyramid, The Paper Men, Rites of Passage* and its sequels, are presented from the third person point of view. In *Lord of the Flies* the whole story is seen from Ralph's point of view. It is only at the end that we are made to contemplate upon the several meanings of the tale by looking at it from the Naval Officer's point of view. *The Inheritors* is an account of devastation seen from the point of view of the exterminated. The limited perception of the New People, who bring about the destruction, informs of a mode of dramatic irony that is steadily and powerfully effective. In the last chapter of the novel, Golding reverses the point of view and establishes a new irony as New Man, fleeing his own inner darkness, looks back in terror at the forest of innocence. The symbolic action of Pincher Martin, seen from the point of view of the protagonist, makes moral points about man's attitudes towards death as they affect his attitude towards life. But a sudden shift towards the end reveals that the entire novel took place in the mind of the drowning man. In *Free Fall* and *The Paper Men,* the conscious and the unconscious are presented directly through a first person narrative, revealing that man lives at an intersection of two incompatible worlds, both of which they must inhabit. The action of *The Spire,* though presented from the third person point of view, is steeped in the inner consciousness of the protagonist involving the realization of a vision and the cost of the vision in human terms. *The Pyramid,* presented from the point of view of Oliver, reveals how an individual's activities are determined to an alarming degree, by external pressures, especially by those of the social order. In *Darkness Visible* Matty's view, in the first part, is balanced against Sophy's view in the second part while the novel ends with the experiences of Sim and Edwin in the third part. In *Rites of Passage* and its sequels we are made to share Talbot's guilt and shame through his first person account of the happenings in the ship which serves as a social microcosm. Through the complex structure and multiple points of view in Golding's fiction, we are made to have a glimpse of his intricate world and its inconsistencies. As Virginia Tiger has rightly pointed out,

> It is not the least of the difficulty in reading Golding that he expects his readers to reassemble narrative images, reconcile apparently opposing points of view, build bridges between contradictory perspective — all in the service of imaginatively participating in his religious construct.[23]

Golding's unusual technique, specially in the use of language and the use of the point of view, have emerged as the means of discovering, exploring, developing, and evaluating the complex subjects of his novels.

With his concern for truth, his powerful imagination, his poetic intensity, his great technical range and his cosmic awareness, Golding has emerged as one of the most powerful writers of contemporary British fiction.

ENDNOTES

1. Virginia Tiger, *The Dark Field of Discovery,* Marion Boyars, London, 1974 , 15.
2. Walter Allen, *Tradition and Dream,* Phoenix House, London, 1964,203.
3. Angus Wilson, 'Evil in the English Novel', *Kenyon Review* 29, March, 1967, 167.
4. William Golding, 'Belief and Creativity' *A Moving Target,* Faber, London, 1982, 199
5. Frank Kermode, 'The Novels of William Golding' *International Literary Annual,* 3, 1961, 21.
6. William Golding, *Radio Times.* (As quoted by B.L. Chakoo in his book *William Golding Revisited,* Arnold Publishers, 1989).
7. James Baker, 'An Interview with William Golding', *Twentieth Century Literature,* 1982 (Summer Issue), 134-35.
8. 'Pincher Martin', *Radio Times,* CXXVIII (March 21, 1958), 8.
9. *Ibid.,* 133-34.
10. Peter Green, The World of William Golding', *Golding's Novels,* ed. Norman Page, Macmillan, 1985, 96.
11. *Op. cit.,* 155.
12. *Op. cit.,* 131.
13. William Golding, 'Fable', *The Hot Gates,* Faber, 1965, 88.
14. Ian Gregor, " He Wondered' : The religious imagination of William Golding", William Golding : The Man and His Books, ed. John Carey, Faber, 1986, 86.
15. 'William Golding : An Interview', *Quorto Magazine,* Vol.11, No. 12, November 1980, 11.
16. 'William Golding, 'Fable', *The Hot Gates,* 89.

17. *Ibid.*, 89.
18. *Op. cit.*, 160.
19. *Ibid.*. 168.
20. Mark Kinkead - Weekes and Ian Gregor, *William Golding : A Critical Study*, Faber, London, 1967, 240.
21. Frank Kermode, 'The Novels of William Golding', *International Literary Annual*, No. 3, 1961.
22. Karl, F., 'The Novel as Moral Allegory', *The Reader's Guide to Contemporary English Novel*, Farrer, 1962, 254.
23. Virginia Tiger, "William Golding's 'Wooden World'", *Twentieth Century Literature*, 1982 (Summer Issue), 218.

2

A Diseased Situation: *The Pyramid*

Shifting scope from the wider horizons of his earlier books, Golding has concentrated more on social realism in his later fiction depicting, simultaneously, the essential human predicament. While focusing attention on the English provincial life, he has portrayed in *The Pyramid* the pernicious effects of class-standards, snobbery , exploitation, hatred, and egotism. He has created a world which is reduced to the immediately observable. *The Pyramid* is not a fable and is not set in a remote or simplified world. It belongs more to the commonplace tradition of English fiction. Devoid of ambiguity and mystery, it portrays the respectability and genteel passions of a very English town. Describing humorously the growth of a young man Oliver in a small English town, he reveals the agony, the pathos, and the tragedy of human beings under the veneer of civilization. The tragedy underlying the comic and the farcical situations is the outcome of a lack of understanding and love amongst the inmates of a class-ridden society. Unable to forget the social class in which he had grown up, Golding endeavours to point out the difficulty of loving spontaneously in such a society. Giving an account of that society in an interview he observed:

> It was about as stratified a society as you could well find anywhere in the country, and I think that the pyramidal structure of English society is present, and my awareness of it is indelibly imprinted in me , in my psyche, not merely in my intellect but very much in my emotional, almost my physical being. I am enraged by it and I am unable to escape it entirely, though obviously as I get older and also as I get better known I have less and less cause to worry about whether I am middle- class, lower middle-class, lower (lower) middle class. . . . It dissolves but it doesn't disappear; it's fossilized in me. [1]

Oliver, the protagonist, reviewing his childhood and adolescence, through three separate episodes, is driven towards truth, and an understanding of man. Though disapproving of the society replete with hypocrisy, corruption, and deceit, he unconsciously begins to share its norms.

The three-fold structure of Stilbourne's social pyramid is indicated by the title itself. While discussing the symbolism of the title of *The Pyramid,* Nicola C. Dicken Fuller, has thus observed:

> The title of *The Pyramid* symbolizes the social pyramid in which Oliver moves. Each of the three sides symbolizes one aspect of his life in Stilbourne, as it is touched by a relationship with another person: Evie Babbacombe, Evelyn De Tracy and Miss Dawlish . . . as the pyramid of time revolves , the end leads back to the beginning . . . Symbolically, Olive r may be viewed as being at the apex of the pyramid, being touched or influenced by each of the three sides.[2]

Three persons endeavour to interact but fail to live owing to the rigidity of the class system. Through the three sections of the novel, Oliver is seen examining introspectively the experiences of his childhood, adolescence, and middle age and is driven towards self-knowledge. The first section is concerned with the adolescent Oliver diverting his frustrated infatuation for Imogen Grantley into lust for Evie Babbacombe. The second section, taking place on his return from Oxford at the end of his first term, reveals Stilbourne's comical attempts at enacting a musical opera, while the third section depicts Oliver coming to Stilbourne as a successful man of the world, recalling his childhood memories concerning his music teacher Bounce Dawlish. Balanced against his passion for music is his class-consciousness, and the three episodes, while dealing with his craving for sex and music, and a desire to hitch himself up on the social ladder, reveal, in contrast, the hypocritical attitudes of his society.

In the first section of the novel, Oliver's lust for Evie is in sharp contrast with his infatuation for Imogen Grantley. Engaged to Norman Claymore, the owner of *The Stilbourne Advertiser,* Imogen Grantley is, for Oliver, the symbol of perfection. Conscious of his position as the dispenser's son, Oliver had never before spoken to Evie who, was the Town Crier's daughter and came from the tumbledown cottages of Chandler's Close' (13). Although the 'local phenomenon', Evie had, according to Oliver, 'none of Imogen's sacred beauty. She was strictly secular'. (16) While he feels superior to Evie in respect of his position, at the same time he is undermined by Bobby Ewans who, being the son of the doctor, is envied not only for his position but also for his motor bike, boarding school education, his profile like that of the Duke of Wellington, and his ability to fight like a boxer. His social antenna working perfectly, Oliver assesses their relative position in the following manner:

> My cliff was as adamant as the Ewans's; but not as high. No, not nearly as high. It was not as high, for example, as the cliff that separated Evie herself, from the louts who hung round the Town Hall, out of work. For Evie, I was a lightning conductor.(60)

Conscious of his position, Oliver wants to improve it by going to Oxford. Though it did not make him as attractive, in Evie's eyes, as Bobby Ewans who was preparing for a glamours career in the air- force, he manages to get her attention. Rescuing the car, used by Bobby and Evie to go to a local dance, from a pond, Oliver attains Evie. While his attention is fixed upward on Imogen

Grantley, he looks upon Evie only as an object of sex. Seducing Evie to satisfy his adolescent lust, Oliver is careful to keep his relations with her a secret. He knows instinctively what detrimental effect his supposed marriage with Evie may have on his parents:

> It would kill them. To be related even if only by marriage, to *Sergeant Babbacombe*! I saw their social world. So delicately poised and carefully maintained, so fiercely defended, crash into the gutter. I should drag them down and down through those minute degrees where it was impossible to rise but always easy to fall. (82)

While Oliver is careful to be secretive, Evie is determined to expose him, first by forcing him out of the woods and then, much later, revealing loudly in the pub about his raping her when she was only fifteen. On returning to Stilbourne from London, for a short while, Evie searches for a person who is alive to human emotions. Looking around the square (symbolizing the square base of a pyramid used to house dead bodies) she says: 'There must be *someone*! Someone alive! (105). Oliver, or any other person is Stilbourne, is incapable of loving genuinely and is dead in Evie's eyes. Accusing him of his failure to outgrow his class prejudice, she says: 'You! Aren't you ever going to grow up ? This place — You. You an' your mum and dad. Too good for people aren't you? · · · (110).

Imprisoned in the repressive society of Stilbourne, its inmates are isolated and sadistic. Evie and Miss Dawlish, with their life-long desire to be loved, are frustrated. Getting very little sympathy from either Oliver or Bobby Ewans, Evie exclaims in contempt and disgust : "You wouldn't care if I was dead. Nobody'd care. That's all you want, just my damned body, . . . never loved me, nobody never loved me. I wanted to be loved, I wanted somebody to be kind to me" (88-89). The lack of genuine love in Oliver gives rise to desire for illicit sex and superficial respectability. Breathing 'perpetual sex', Evie, for him, is 'life's necessary, unspeakable object'. (91)

Though the craving for Evie had become overpowering, the class standards of Stilbourne impinged upon Oliver the incorrectness of such a desire. Waiting desperately to meet her, he thinks and dreams of her. By Stilbourne standards, he knew it was 'wrong' to pine for a girl belonging to a class much lower than his as is made apparent by his dream:

> I had settled from terror to a state of continual worry. My dreams had a new dread; and always the same thing. I dreamed I was walking about Stilbourne, but condemned to death. My parents were in the dream — indeed all the people of Stilbourne were there and all concurred in the death sentence since my crime, which the dream left vague, was unpardonable. (84)

Oliver finds himself torn between two worlds, the clean coloured one of his parents and Imogen, on the one hand, and the hateful but necessary one of Evie who was '[the] object, on an earth that smelt of decay, with picked bones and natural cruelty— lifes lavatory'. (91)

Coming to know of Oliver's connection with Evie, his father is concerned more with his son's health than with Evie's depression as a result of an exploitation of her by some of the Stilbourne men. Though making up 'prescriptions for all the ailments of Stilbourne' (100), Oliver's father knows of no treatment for the class disease. At-tributing Oliver's lust for Evie to the 'books-cinema- papers- this sex . . .' (100) he considers it to be all wrong. Oliver, too, believes Evie to be one of the diseases his father talks about.

Living in a world of self-delusion, it is only much later that Oliver has a glimpse of the real Evie. Discovering his assumptions regarding Evie to be baseless, he is led from incomprehension to enlightenment. With a shock he realizes that not only has her innocence been destroyed at the age of fifteen, but that she has been a victim of her father's sadistic desires too. He says:

> I stood, in shame and confusion, seeing for the first time despite my anger a different picture of Evie in her

> life-long struggle to be clean and sweet. It was as if this object of frustration and desire had suddenly acquired the attributes of a person rather than a thing . (111)

The concretely demarcated class-structure of Stilbourne causes misunderstanding and leads to a breakdown of communication among its inmates.

In the middle section of the book, the absurdity of the middle class respectability is brought forth forcefully to Oliver through the performance of the *King of Hearts* by the Stilbourne Operatic Society. All Stilbourne values, too, are ludicrously exposed. Forced into taking part, Oliver is a participant as well as an observer with his judgment called into play. He has a growing awareness of the hollowness behind the social life, and the meaninglessness of some of its values. The performance by the SOS releases the emotions which are otherwise suppressed by society. As Oliver says,

> With diabolical inevitability, the very desires to act and be passionate, to show off and impress, brought to full flower the jealousies and hatreds, meannesses and indignations we were forced to conceal in ordinary life. (114)

Evelyn de Tracy, the effeminate producer of the *King of Hearts*, while appearing very condescending and full of flattery initially, is quite matter of fact and plain- spoken later and enlightens Oliver about Imogen for whom he has an infatuation. For the first time he is made to see the 'stupid, insensitive, vain woman' that she is with a 'neat face and just enough sense to keep smiling' (145-46). Contrasted with his earlier view of Imogen as a perfect woman is his realization of her insensitivity as a singer. Oliver is shocked to notice that Imogen accepts the lead role in the operetta in spite of her inability to sing. As he says:

> She had walked indifferently into a Country to which I had access, of which indeed, I was native. In that landscape where notes of music, and all sounds were

> visible, coloured things, she trod with ignorant, ungainly feet. It was not just that she could not sing. It was that she was indifferent to the fact that she could not sing; and yet had gone, consenting to this public exhibition. She was so out of tune that the line of song that should have been spiky as a range of mountains was worn down like a line of chalk hills, (154)

Playing the lead role against Imogen is her husband, Norman Claymore, who is as ignorant, vain, and self-absorbed as his wife. The play becomes a farce with the actors vieing with each other for supremacy, revealing their pettiness, jealousy, and snobbery. Even the music they practice is sung in thin gnat-like voices. Evelyn helps Oliver see everything for what it is. Liberated from the closed walls of his world, Oliver exclaims in disgust :

> Everything's — *wrong*. Everything. There's no truth and there's no honesty. My God! Life can't — I mean just out there, you have only to look up at the sky - - but Stilbourne accepts it as a *roof*. As a — and the way we hide our bodies and the things we don't say, the things we daren't mention, the people we don't meet - - and that *stuff* they call music — it's a lie! Don't they understand ? It's a lie, a lie ! It's —obscene! (147)

Class-consciousness is much more starkly exposed through the performance of the play where the actors are chosen from a handful of people 'round whom an invisible line was drawn. Nobody mentioned the line, but everybody knew it was there' (114). While the leading roles had to be given to the important personages of Stilbourne, people from the lower rung could not qualify, even if they had the qualities. Neither her ability to sing, nor her beauty could qualify Evie even for a minor role as she was the Town Crier's daughter and came from Chandler's Close. Though Mrs. Underhill had a voice which sounded like 'a patient in a nearby hospital', and Mr. Claymore sounded like a gnat, they got the prominent roles because the former was the Mayor's daughter and the latter the owner of Stilbourne's only newspaper. The dehumanizing nature of class differences is exposed with the ludicrous argument between Mr. Claymore and Oliver's mother regarding what Oliver should be called by the former in the play. While Mr. Claymore expresses a desire to call him 'My man', Oliver's mother insists on 'General'. The argument ends with both compromising on 'Captain'.

Mr. Evelyn de Tracy, with his 'moony smile', constantly shaking legs which have a 'tendency to move side-ways at the knee', yellowing eyeballs, minute pupils, and a tiny black tuft of hair on top of his head, has a suggestion of the good and the evil overlapping in his person, and serves to expose the Stilbourne values. The pettiness of the people of Stilbourne is revealed through the contrast between the gnat-like voices of the inmates of Stilbourne, and the natural, booming, though gentle, voice of Evelyn. Dressed as a comic character sometimes and sometimes as a ballerina, Evelyn knows more about Imogen, particularly because of the woman in him. As his name signifies, he is half-woman and half-man. When Oliver demands to know the truth Evelyn produces some photographs which reveal him dressed as a ballerina, supported by another young man. Oliver is not perceptive enough to understand the meaning of the photographs and has fits of uncontrolled laughter. Though the truth of Evelyn being a homosexual stares him in the face, he cannot understand it. Coaxing and humouring everybody, he has no illusions about their basic character. Thus, for him, life is an 'outrageous farce . . . with an incompetent producer' (148). Evelyn was a spectator with an unusual view of the world which was a stage where new dramas were being enacted daily and his view of Stilbourne was only 'the last in a whole series of private entertainments' (155). Before putting him in the last bus to Barchester, Oliver sees him hanging by the sharp points of the iron railings around the Square, signifying the prison of the pyramid. Evelyn decidedly wanted to leave this prison of Stilbourne even before the end of the play he was producing. Surrounded by mist of incomprehension, he remains an enigma for Oliver. After having enlarged Oliver's consciousness and contributed to his education, Evelyn disappears from Stilbourne.

Moving back and forth through Oliver's consciousness, which is illuminated gradually, we glimpse into the working of the human soul trapped within the boundaries of a rigid society. Though understanding the pathetic nature of Bounce's condition, Oliver is incapable of removing her sufferings because of his conditioning by the Stilbourne society which, being insensitive to an individual's needs, fosters cruelty. In the third section of the book, Oliver as a grown up man tries to understand the influence of Stilbourne's society in bringing about the sad end of Bounce's life, by recapturing the incidents of his childhood in which Bounce occupied an important position as his music teacher. Bounce's father, believing that 'Heaven is Music', proves to be a tyrannical father who is insensitive to his daughter's needs. Like Oliver's parents, he has his own will with his child and forces her to sacrifice all earthly pleasures for the sake of music which he himself is incapable of understanding thoroughly. Bounce gives an account of her father's treatment of her to Oliver:

> When I was a girl my father made me copy out fugues with a different coloured ink for each voice; and if I got a part wrong – Crack! went his ruler across my knuckles . . . Bonk! In the organ loft with a roll of music- Jab ! in the ribs with the point of a bow. (171)

Forced to take up a career in music, Bounce not only failed to enjoy it but also made mistakes while practicing or teaching. Putting her fingers in the 'wrong places' (168), while teaching violin, she made her pupils laugh. Often falling asleep, while her students practiced, she attempted to escape the drudgery of music. Though accepting music as the ultimate goal in life, and being forced to be dedicated to it, Bounce could not play. That she is unconscious of the fact that she cannot play becomes quite apparent to Oliver when she plays a Chopin Impromptu all wrong.

Not only is Bounce a failure in music, her attempts to be loved also remain fruitless. Henry William's arrival, as her car mechanic, brings a ray of light in the gloom of her lonely life. But being concerned more with materialistic aspirations, Henry makes strict demarcations with regard to giving her love. She is exploited for money. Ignoring Bounce's repeated protests, work is carried on noisily in the garage which he makes with her money, interrupting the music lessons she gives her students. Her pathetic pleading, 'All I want is for you to need me, need me' (195), go unheeded. Failing to receive love from Henry, Bounce gets involved in regular squabbles with his family. Because bitter and cynical, she is filled with disgust for human beings and says: 'If I could save a child or a budgie from a burning home, I'd save the budgie' (212). Driven to desperation she makes and exhibition of her desire by walking naked through the streets of Stilbourne.

Like Henry, Oliver, too, fails in giving any affection to Bounce. He is guided by the double standards of Stilbourne's society in showing a devoted exterior while, in reality, being totally devoid of feeling. As he grows up, he can analyse his attitude: 'I could only just bear ingratiating exterior and the unvoiced thoughts and unanalysable feelings that flittered behind it' (188). Being afraid of her as a child, he develops a strong aversion to her. Standing in front of her grave, he admits : 'I never liked you ! Never !' Fostering hypocrisy, society breeds men who measure human relations in terms of money. Oliver realized that like Henry he, too, would never pay more than a reasonable price for anything. Looking at Henry's eyes, he sees his own face. Driven by the desire to accumulate wealth and respectability, Oliver sacrifices his musical career choosing chemistry as a means of earning money. Suspecting this attitude in Henry and Oliver, Bounce advises the latter with bitterness : 'Don't be a musician, Kummer, my son. Go into the garage business if you want to make money' (193). That the idea of becoming a professional musician is shameful is inculcated in him year after year by his parents. Therefore, regulated more by the demands of society, Oliver is afraid of pursuing what his heart desires. A class conscious society like Stilbourne's fosters misunderstanding, resulting in a lack of communication. Though curious about others' affairs, the inmates of Stilbourne lack genuine sympathy for each other. Living in houses with 'railed off enclosure', 'spring locked doors', and windows with impenetrable curtains, they desist from direct interaction. Oliver, recording his childhood perceptions, finds the women more curious and subtle in this regard than the men. As he writes:

> Standing back about a yard inside these curtains, they sent out what I should now call a kind of radar emission which was reflected from each other's business. A curious element appears in this; that to a certain extent the emission was capable of piercing a curtain, so that to a woman, each family was dimly visible, while each thought itself protected.(177)

Rotating in their own small worlds, they fail to touch each other emotionally. Taking interest in others' affairs only to criticize and castigate, they tend to force people like Bounce to live in isolation and a dark emptiness, turning them into eccentrics. Failing to receive any affection from human beings, Bounce finds solace in the company of animals like cats and birds.

In *The Pyramid*, Golding has deftly pointed out that when a society begins to lay emphasis more on material success than love, understanding, and fellow-feeling, then there occur increased cases of insanity resulting from frustration. Just as in *Free Fall* Beatrice becomes mad when ignored by Sammy after being exploited physically by him, Bounce, too, is pushed into the abyss of insanity when she fails to receive love from Henry, and is similarly exploited for wealth by him. Neither does Evie receive any true love from Ewans or Oliver. Exploited for her body, she, too, would have met the same fate as Bounce's, hadn't she escaped from Stilbourne. A society without love tends to become a place for the dead like a pyramid. The inmates become architects of their own tragedy not knowing when they need catharsis. The only way left for Oliver is to escape and not think about the inmates of Stilbourne.

By juxtaposing three stories, whose tones are varied, Golding has stressed the derogatory quality of class divisions. Oliver, the narrator, while recapturing his childhood, adolescence, and middle age, presents the story with considerable vivacity and sharpness of detail. Ian Gregor has compared it with a comedy of manners.

As he says: 'The comedy of manners, which itself is varied throughout the novel, is associated in the first story with irony, in the second more with farce, and in the third with tragedy.'[3] Oliver's consciousness travels through the technique of flashback and flashforwards revealing his transition and mode of visualization. The three stories are represented from Oliver's point of view. The first story registers his adolescent excitements and feelings, and is ironical as he can hardly fathom what he sees. While the second story is farcical with Evelyn becoming a means for revealing Stilbourne's pretensions, the third is nearer to tragedy, depicting loneliness, isolation, and estrangement.

Music plays an important role in the three sections of the novel. While talking of its form, Golding said in an interview :

> It is sonata form really, it's musical. With a Scherzo in the middle, the whole business about the idiotic amateur dramatic director is the scherzo of the sonata, and then it finishes with a Beethoven set of variations . . . . [4]

Music is the unifying factor of the novel. While in the first section Oliver's adolescent passion, his trials and tribulations, are expressed through his playing the piano, in the second section the musical opera becomes a means of revealing the people of Stilbourne, and the third section depicts what place music has in shaping the lives of Oliver and Bounce. Frustration leads Bounce to burn her music books and instruments as a sign of repudiation of all that her father emphasized as important. Instead of bringing harmony and happiness in her life, the practice of music brings only discord and despair. Music, by contrast, brings out the unhappiness and dissatisfaction in the lives of the inmates of Stilbourne. For Oliver, music has other connotations. As he says:

> I had discovered the emotional confir-mations and enlargements of music, not as a supposition, but as a fact of experience; and though I still endured the violin I had fallen in love with the piano and was bashing the last use out of our tinny upright (188).

While Oliver, who understands music better than Bounce and wants to take it seriously as his career, is discouraged, Bounce taking it seriously, proves to be a failure.

The work may also be called a black comedy with the comic and the tragic intermingling. The deft light touches in the first and the second sections reveal the comic side of life. Though predominantly gloomy, the third section has comic moments when Oliver recounts the behaviour of Stilbourne women, his mother being one of them. The use of young Oliver by his mother as 'a kind of interplanetary probe' (177), to collect information about the neighbours and their activities becomes a source of comedy mingled with irony. At times, comedy is used to reveal the darker side of Bounce's life. Oliver's fear of music lessons and his wish to go home are mistaken for his desire to attend to nature's call. Bounce leads him through dark corridors, angled stairs, and shadowy passages to the toilet. The primary, ignorant perceptions of the child, when examined with an adult's experience, reveal ironically the dark and the gloomy aspect of her life:

> She handed me the candlestick and shut the door behind me. I advanced fear – fully and saw a water closet of brown earthenware. Beside it was a handle and an iron rod which went straight up, miles up, through the ceiling. Behind me, I heard Bounce's manly shoes clump away down the corridor. I backed against the wall, and concen-trated as hard as I could on the flame of the candle. I could understand now how I had mistaken her meaning and she, mine; . . . I stayed where I was against the wall and the ice of that darkness and remoteness formed on my skin and in my hair. (169-170)

Misinterpretation and lack of communication create chasms which become unbridgeable.

Golding's preoccupation with the divisiveness of class and its direct consequence finds expression first in the *The Pyramid*, and later in the trilogy of *Rites of Passage*. Whereas the protagonist of

The Pyramid cannot grow out of his prejudices, Talbot is seen discarding his biased nature and metamorphosing into a wholesome being in the trilogy. Contrasted with the earlier novels which are concerned with the philosophical, *The Pyramid* depicts the contemporary social milieu much more concretely. Though its characters fail to live up to the truth pointed out in the epigraph of the novel, the protagonists of *Darkness Visible* and the trilogy strive to realize it. The complexities arising out of the narrow-mindedness of a society resistant to change as depicted in *The Pyramid* can be simplified only through love, as is shown by Matty in *Darkness Visible.*

ENDNOTES

1. '*The Guardian*', 11 Oct. 1980. 12.
2. Nicola C. Dicken-Fuller, *William Golding's Use of Symbolism,* The Book Guild Ltd, Sussex England, 1990, 38.
3. Mark Kinkead – Weakes and Ian Gregor, *William Golding.* Faber, 1984, 264.
4. James Baker, *An Interview.* 153.

3

The Process of Change: *The Scorpion God*

The three constituent novellas of *The Scorpion God,* viz., *The Scorpion God, Clonk Clonk* and *Envoy Extraordinary* written at different times and concerned with separate societies, are semi-didactic, put together and brought out in the form of a book 'wide and big enough to be put on sale',[1] they have very little in common. Enjoyable as they are, the three novellas cannot be counted as major works of fiction. With their settings variously in ancient Egypt, prehistoric times, and imperial Rome, the tales take one back to the dark past. The collection is named after the first story which depicts Golding's perennial interest in Egypt. As he admitted in an interview, '. . . I had the Egyptology up my sleeve all the time. I was quite sure I was going to write something about it sooner or later'.[2] Ancient society, almost the beginning of political history, is Golding's theme in his lightly satiric novella *The Scorpion God.* Here, as admitted in an interview, Golding was sending up the idea of history.[3] The author who is perennially interested in Egypt has recreated the culture of pre-dynastic Egypt in *The Scorpion God.* The story ends at a point when a change takes place in the history of Egypt with the dynastic rule of a Pharaoh ending and a new ruler called the Scorpion, taking his place. Uniting the whole of Egypt and making many innovations, the digging of artificial channels being one of them, Scorpion becomes a powerful ruler. Explaining the historical background of the story and his motive in choosing the particular title Golding says:

> . . . the first recorded Pharaoh, the one who united the whole of Egypt, united upper and lower Egypt, was called Menes. Now, I don't know what that name means, but there was another Pharaoh and there's a huge Egyptological argument going on as to whether the name Scorpion, which they found on a slate palette, is an alternative name for this chapter, or whether it is an unknown Pharaoh before him. I choose to make the Scorpion Pharaoh the one who unites the whole of Egypt, so when the dying high priest says 'he stings like a scorpion,' that names the Pharaoh. He is going to unite Egypt, make it a great power. He's Nothing like an Egyptian at all. And So he is Scorpion, and he is God. There was a 'Scorpion God'.[4]

Golding, while preoccupied with the dark part of human nature, is confronted with questions concerning life and death. Ancient Egypt, with her relics and arts, while answering some of his questions, touches the very core of his being. Admitting his spiritual connection with Egypt he says:

> My link with the Egyptians is deep and sure. I do not believe them either wise or foolish. I am, in fact, an ancient Egyptian, with all their unreason, spiritual pragmatism and capacity for ambiguous and even contradictory belief.[5]

Being always interested in the mystery surrounding death, Golding found a kindred soul amongst the Egyptians who, while being greatly pre-occupied with death, were always conscious of its co-existence with life. For them, 'It [was] to be at once alive and dead; to suggest mysteries with no solution, to mix the strange, the gruesome and the beautiful'.[6] The Egyptian mummy, symbolizing the Egyptians' grasp of infinity, seemed to dwell with a darkness that was its light. While being 'timelessly frozen and intimidating', the mummy was 'an eternal question mark'. To look into its eyes, Golding is convinced, is to have knowledge of death and meet death itself.

The Scorpion God, vividly portraying some of the beliefs and rituals of the Egyptian people, presents a moment in the history of Egypt when the old order changed giving place to a new. The incidents project a picture of ancient Egypt, but do not present historical events accurately. Golding's own views on this point are stated thus:

> To some extent, I'm sending up the idea of history, and have tongue in my cheek much more often than people ever suspect because I have this kind of solemn reputation . My tongue is in my cheek an awful lot of the time, and it was in those stories, it was tucked in there firmly.[7]

The locale of the story is the Egypt of the time just prior to the period when a king of the upper kingdom of the Nile conquers the lower kingdom and establishes his capital at Memphis. While portraying the time just before the end of the dynastic rule in Egypt, it reveals the people's insularity, and rational attitude to life. The king, supposed to be the incarnation of God, is believed to have powers for making the fruitful, for raising the waters of the river to promote good crops, and for holding the sky aloft. Believed to be the source of life, health and strength, his ability is proved in his running successfully around his fields once in seven years and copulating with his daughter publicly. For the Egyptians, living in a world of their own, cut off from the rest of the world, incest is intrinsic, and sex relation with those outside the family, unnatural and sinful. Failing, first, to complete the race and, second, to perform the obligatory copulation with his daughter Pretty Flower, the king has to enter his eternal life by taking poison. After elaborate preparations he is buried along with the necessary domestics and chosen representatives of the main professions. While all drink poison willingly to accompany their God to the Now in the House of Life, the Liar, the most favoured one, refuses eternal life. Shocked and bewildered by this refusal, the Head Man sends the liar to the pit as he is 'unclean and must be cleaned' (40).

The King's failure to accomplish his duty, and the continued rise of the river waters are linked up, by the Head Man, with Pretty Flower's illicit relations with the Liar and also with the Liar's refusal to accompany the king in his motionless Now. The only solution to this crisis would be to force the Liar to join his master. After being retrieved from the pit, he is asked by the Head Man, to drink poison. While resisting vehemently, he demands to be treated like the King but is ordered, instead, by the Head man to be killed. In desperation the Liar kills the soldiers, wounds the Head Man, and dives into the river for safety. Amazed at the Liar's lust for life in this world, insignificant in comparison with the eternal life, the Head Man cannot help making a last statement: 'He has a death wish' (62). Perhaps sensing the possibility of the Liar's becoming the next king, the prince asks his sister pretty Flower : 'Then my eyes wouldn't matter, and I wouldn't have to be a God, would I? (61)

The story primarily reveals a clash between a rationalist and a man of imagination. The Head Man, believing man to be distinct from the rest of the creation for 'his capacity to look at facts - - and draw from them a conclusion' (50), is himself a rationalist and an empiricist. Believing only in the existence of that which can be seen he takes the Liar's stories to be fantasies while considering him to be mad: 'A madman whose lies have — for all of us — stirred up the central, unspeakable plenum; a madman who is a peril to us all unless he agrees to serve the God' (55). On the other hand, the Liar, while considering himself to be the only sensible man in a land of half wits, cannot understand why models of men cannot be used to accompany the god in his last journey or why people cannot climb the nearby hill to escape the spate of the river. Understanding present life to be much more precious than the eternal one, he does not flinch from taking forcibly the old man's food and water while imprisoned in the pit. With this cunning, farsightedness, and ambition, he realizes what unlimited power a man could have at his disposal if he became the king. Thinking aloud he says:

> The man who holds the high seat in this country is the man who has [pretty Flower], strange and beautiful woman, for his bed. He could burn up the banks of this river from one end to the other, until all men living by it were bowing to [her] beauty. (60)

Ambition soaring high, he questions the Head Man: 'Supposing I were Great House' (60). Though ordered to be killed, the ruthless and self-interested Liar kills the Head Man and ushers in a new age in Egypt.

That a rationalist's limited perspective often fails to explain the mysterious and the unknown is made apparent through the Head Man's inability to explain things rightly and by his tendency to discuss things that cannot be explained as the creation of imagination. His belief that the stories told by the Liar cannot be real but only 'a desperate attempt'. Religious orthodoxy and limited perspective is to be counted by the ability to think freely. While every thought and judgment of the Headman is constrained by his limited view point, making him incapable of thinking far into the future, the Liar's ability to stretch his mind to the farthest limit and guage the danger inherent in the practices and customs of his people enables him to become a powerful king of Egypt as signified by the title of the novella.

Grieved by man's sinful nature and his debasement in modern society, Golding tries to recapture the innocence and the peace of primeval times in *Clonk Clonk*, the second novella in the collection. Golding is an advocate of man's Edenic conciousness and, as in *The Inheritors*, in *Clonk Clonk*, too, he depicts man in a state still unfallen and innocent. But while *The Inheritors* is pessimistic in out look, *Clonk Clonk* ends on an optimistic note. The matriarchal society depicted in *Clonk Clonk* is set at the beginning of civilizations, a time when community living was prevalent — all the men living at one place and the women at another. A woman could take a companion at will. The general belief being that the children were a gift of the Sky Woman, the children did not know who their father was, though Palm's guess is that she bore children only when she had a male companion. Contrasted with world of the Neanderthals, which is threatened with extinction, the society of the African tribe in *Clonk Clonk* is free from worries, and has no hostile enemies. While the women collect honey, roots, fruits, eggs, and leaves, make alcohol, and look after the children and the aged, the men hunt animals and kill birds for feathers. Though teasing and making fun of the weak one is common sport amongst the men, their pastime never tends to be violent. Innocent, and fun-loving like children, they never hurt each other with their weapons. Driven away from their company temporarily because of his weak ankle and blunders, Chimp is welcomed back into the group. Enjoying a close bond of fellow-feeling, the men tend to be homosexual when away from home. To them love is unselfconscious as sleep:

> They put off weapons so that there was a scattered jumble before the splayed roots. They snuggled, old and young together into the natural rest places between the roots so that the trunk seemed to grow a frill of brown skin and sliding muscles. The dappled shade shifted over them. The singing became a crooning, murmuring sound as they hugged and cuddled and made love. There was much stroking and intimate sharing till heat and satisfaction sunk them towards sleep. (78)

A sense of joyous harmony pervades the camp of the women, too, while they are more capable and responsible than the men. Laughing and chattering, they usually stay in groups except for the time they look after the children. While drinking alcohol ritually after a naming ceremony, the women become drunk and boisterous and do not like the hunters to find them in that condition. Though physically weaker than the men, the women dominate and regulate the life of their society treating men as children.

Revealing the lives of men and women living in groups, the story delineates the inner life of two individuals — Palm and

Chimp. Palm, variously called She-who-names-the-women, Namer-of-women, She-whose-heart-is-loaded- down-with-names, is distinct from the others not only for her acute perceptions but also for her place of authority both among women and men. Sensitive to the natural objects around her — the mountain, the moon, the river water and their own habitation — she can intuitively feel what each actually is. She is haunted by the feeling that the mountain looking up at the sky or staring down at them is oblivious of their presence. Having the capacity to look at things objectively and assess their value, she observes the moon and feels:'The Sky Woman is just the Sky Woman. That is all. To think anything else is to be young' (92). Or while observing the men's lodge:

> She saw the lodge for what it was, without the distortion of contempt or humour or caution. It was a pan like all the others but empty of water . . . her moment of seeing was as clear and precise as if she had woken from a dream and found nothing but the factual straws by her cheek. (92)

Always smiling, caressing, and consoling, she is the epitome of womanhood. While in a deeply dejected and helpless mood, Chimp gets consolation from her and feels revived.

Sensitive and emotional, Chimp, when driven away from the company of the hunting group, can imagine his two selves — one with the group and the other, the real one, in seclusion. Overpowered by loneliness, he has sensations which the others, as a group, do not perceive:

> Feelings swelled in his belly as if he were with child of them. They over-whelmed. He lifted up his voice and howled at the mountains and the Sky Woman, at the forests and the plain, as if he were not a Leopard man but a dog . . . Then, as if something had come to be born , the feelings were clear in their message. They gave him a knowledge, a certainty. (98-99)

In his distraught condition he turns to the place of women for comfort. Though initially terrorized by their drinking orgy, he receives consolation and love from the maternal and protective Palm and is finally accepted as her husband and as a Leopard Man.

The society, when still controlled by women, is free from the terrors of violence. Being more evolved than men in thought and sensitivity, women are successful in keeping the peace and harmony of their community. It is indicative of the fact that restraining male aggression in our present world could recapture the lost Eden.

Contrasted with the innocent world of *Clonk Clonk* is the relatively modern world of *Envoy Extraordinary,* the third novella in the collection. Though written in a lighter vein, it reveals Golding's preoccupation with man's proclivity towards evil. Man, through his ingenuity, has invented many things, yet his tendency towards evil induces him to use them for destructive purposes.

The story reveals a Greek inventor, Phanocles, coming to the court of Caesar with his three inventions — a steamship, a pressure cooker, and an explosive missile. Phanocles' mysteriously silent sister Euphrosyne, who accompanies her brother, becomes the object of love of Mamillius, Caesar's grandson. Posthumus, the heir-designate, on receiving news of the steamship and the explosive, rushes back from his campaign suspecting Caesar and Mamillius of conspiring against him. In his attempt to kill Caesar, with the explosive, Posthumus himself is accidentally killed while some of his ships are deranged by Phanocles' steamship. Caesar is grateful for being saved but is suspicious, all the same, of the inventions. Phanocles, on the other hand, having an insight into the secrets of nature, moves in a world of 'substance and force' (128), and knows that he can have his way with the universe. While he is confident of being able to change the universe with Caesar's help, the latter is doubtful about his capacity to improve it for he is suspicious of man's nature. Anything powerful in his hands may be used for changes which are 'almost always for the worse' (130). The pressure cooker is accepted but the steamship, the explosive and the printing press are rejected. Unlike Phanocles, who hopefully believes that the invention of the steamship would set the slaves free, Caesar despairs of human nature and believes that no invention can change the basic conditions. As he says to Phanocles,

> There will always be slaves though the name may change. What is slavery but the domination of the weak by the strong? How can you make them equal? Or are you fool enough to think that men are born equal ? (176)

The suspicion that man has an innate lust for killing is turned into a belief when Caesar, on asking a captain about his enjoying the prospect of a battle, receives the answer : ' On the whole, yes . . . Makes a change. Excitement, promotion, perhaps loot – and so on' (167). Therefore, though the explosive had saved his life and killed Posthumus, it is rejected, for it could thoughtlessly destroy those who could be useful to mankind. The idea of the printing press is not welcomed because of the possibility of its becoming a means of proliferating knowledge. Sensing that a natural philosopher like Phonocles could be a source of danger as he could go as far as 'wiping life off the earth' (173), Caesar sends him off to China as an ambassador.

Golding has tried to drive home the fact that though man has unravelled the secret powers of nature, his inabiiity to control his evil propensities is threatening his very existence on this globe. While man was living relatively peacefully at the beginning of civilization, the progress in knowledge has made him increasingly violent and self-destructive. It is love, sympathy, and understanding for fellow beings which should occupy the place of importance instead of hatred and violence which have transformed the world into a living hell.

While the theme of the first and the last novellas is man's perennial desire to change his existing conditions through personal endeavour or inventions, the second novella *Clonk Clonk* shows man in a relatively harmonious and happy state. Being anthropological fables, they reveal that 'Change . . . is often a matter of accident, circumstances, chance, and . . . the changes or patterns . . . in history are more often a result of coincidence'.[8]

Tied together, the three stories have a unity while taking one back to remote times. Rigidly structured and tightly controlled, they simultaneously have light and deft touches. While *Envoy Extraordinary* has a number of comic moments, *The Scorpion God* has highly poetic passages. The exotic setting, the narrative style and vivid imagination carry one effectively back to the remote times and it never escapes the reader's notice that Golding's constant concern is for man's fallen nature, his inherent depravity, and capacity for evil.

ENDNOTES

1. James Baker 'An Interview with William Golding', 158.
2. *Ibid.,* 160.
3. *Ibid.,* 158.
4. *Ibid.,* 160.
5. William Golding 'Egypt from my Inside' *A Moving Target,* 1982, 55.
6. *Ibid.,* 54.
7. James Baker, *Op. cit.,* 158.
8. *Ibid.,* 158.

4

Probing the Depths: *Darkness Visible*

Darkness Visible, as the Miltonic title suggests, concerns itself with the core of Golding's mystical perception. From the beginning of his literary career, Golding has been preoccupied with the idea of darkness. Darkness, which is absence of light to a scientist, is, to Golding, a looming terror, inexplicable, unexorcised, haunted, a gulf over which one could not reach out to light. It has been Golding's theme for over three decades.

In *Lord of the Flies,* darkness is the experience of the evil side of the human heart. Innocence is sacrificed for the knowledge of dark powers. In *The Inheritors,* the Homo Sapiens, having destroyed the innocent Neanderthals, move towards a future which is dark and uncertain. Golding here highlights evil as emanating from the human mind. In *Pincher Martin,* Pincher's last battle with darkness signifies his battle with the dark night of the soul. In *Free Fall,* through Sammy Mountjoy's ordeal by darkness, when he is kept imprisoned in a dark cell, darkness becomes a source of revelation. If the dark pit in which the cathedral floats is symbolic of the darkness of man's heart in *The Spire,* then the inability to learn in a class conscious society, is a form of death or spiritual darkness in *The Pyramid.* By penetrating the mysteries of the spiritual world that lies hidden, or are ignored by most of us, Golding deals with the same theme in cosmic terms in *Darkness Visible*. Delving deeper and deeper into the workings of the forces of good and evil in the individual and in society, he seeks to make darkness finally visible. The mystery of a world, lying hidden from the common eye, becomes the object of exploration, suggested by the epigraph: 'sit mihi fas audita loque', a line from Virgil's *Aeneid* (6:266) meaning 'may it be allowed to me to speak what I have heard'. Invocation is made to the dark gods by Virgil to make the darkness of the underworld visible through exploration of the abysmal depths. Golding, too, hopes to illuminate the darkness below the surface of contemporary society.

While exhibiting a constant struggle between the good and the evil forces in the world, in *Darkness Visible*, Golding suggests that however debauched contemporary man may be, he has the hope of being granted the possibility of salvation. A fallen man like Pedigree is redeemed through the benevolence and selfless love of a saint like Matty who typifies the bright, the good, and the holy side of human nature. Matty emerges into this world scarred by the inferno raging in the London dockyard — a result of hatred, criminality, aggressiveness, and immorality of modern man. Matty, the epitome of goodness, is contrasted against Sophy in whom the dark powers have a full play. Contrasted with the earlier novels, where saintly figures appear only for a short while, *Darkness Visible* has Matty as the central character who spreads his message of love and sacrifice among fellow beings. As Don Crompton has rightly pointed out,

> The central role given to this strange, other worldly figure and to the final conflict between the forces of darkness and the forces of light in which he is engaged, is at once the mark of the novel's difference from the rest and of its major importance in the canon of Golding's work. Appropriately, in the light of its title, it could be seen as Golding's own *Paradise Lost*, the novel that above all others pleased him 'long choosing and beginning late', and which, in terms of sheer scope

> and endeavour must surely rank with any produced this century.[1]

Incorporating elements of the Old Testament and the New in the portrayal of a twentieth-century world, *Darkness Visible* has become a modern book of Revelation depicting the existence of some spiritual forces which influence, modify, and direct man's environment.

The forces of good and evil are counterbalanced, principally, by two characters. On the one hand is the high-minded, literal, loving, sacrificing, faithful, and saintly Matty who by closely following the Bible, endeavours to establish the kingdom of God on earth. On the other, there is the highly intelligent, nihilistic, cynical, sadistic, and disloyal Sophy, who, through her 'weirdness' and transgression, is bent on destabilizing the forces of good in the cosmos. The confluence of the two brings to surface the eternal struggle between the opposite forces, making one aware of other dimensions.

Darkness Visible seeks to bring back the neglected, almost forgotten, religious dimensions of human experience, to a world confused and dislocated by the ceaseless sounds of jets and juggernauts, by criminality and terrorism. It depicts a clash between the forces of good and evil in a twentieth-century English society. The barrage balloons, searchlights, bombs discovered in the act of falling, and the shameful inhuman lights of the inferno make one vividly conscious of what man has made of his world. The intense religious feelings in part I are contrasted with the evils in part II. With electronic bugging, secret service activities, terrorism, jet planes, television, drugs and rampant sex, *Darkness Visible* has all the materials of a twentieth-century thriller.

As Ian Gregor views,

> Conceived on a massive scale, it seeks to create religious dimensions . . . by asking what does it mean for a writer to have a religious imagination, in the violence of late, twentieth-century life. What in other words will it mean

> to introduce 'a holy man', into a world of global crime and hijacking.[2]

Golding's religious concern, embedded in the very grain of his imagination, inspired him to write a novel which is interspersed with images, incidents, and characters reminiscent of those in the Bible, making it a modern book of Revelation. Matty, before being given a name, is called number 7 which is also the number of the Book of Revelation. His Christian name, Matthew Septimus, (Septimus meaning seven in Latin) suggestive of Matthew, Chapter 7, issues indications of the theme of judgement, the novel's pre-eminent concern. St. Matthew, VII & I reads: 'Judge not, that ye be not judged'. Matty is baptized in fire. The book begins and ends with references to fire recalling the Apocalypse which '. . .provides the most important single reference point for the whole novel.' 3 As in the *Book of Revelation* where there is a clearcut division between Christ and anti-Christ, in *Darkness Visible* this polarization is evinced by Matty and Sophy, one dedicated to the good and the other taking pleasure in evil. The incidents in Matty's life signify his movement from Eden to Apocalypse while undergoing sufferings similar to those of the prophets of the Old Testament. Matty's thoughts and actions are conditioned by his knowledge of the Bible which is his constant companion and guide. When tempted by the flesh he recites the words of the Bible to protect himself. Commenting on the inclusion of Biblical matter in *Darkness Visible*, Don Crompton has rightly observed :

> Golding . . .with considerable virtuosity, incorporates elements of the Bible, from Genesis to Revelation , in his novel so that it seems that some- times deliberately, sometimes accident- tally, Matty acts out a series of biblical roles, himself becoming a changing exemplar of biblical typology. The young boy who limps from hospital, one side of his face destroyed by the fire, has some of the characteristics of Cain in the Genesis story, but even in the first episode at Greenfield a metamorphosis takes place as Matty slips from being

> Cain to Esau, and then takes on some of the characteristics of Moses.[4]

Having followed the Old Testament, the Book of the Law, and the Prophets, for some time Matty is advised, by some spirits, to take up the New Testament. Alternatingly resembling John the Baptist and Christ John, Matty's biblical roles tend to slide into each other and overlap. While Matty has some biblical roles to play, Sophy's role, too, transforms from one that resembles the Whore of Babylon in the Apocalypse to that which becomes synonymous with Satan. Matty's journal, which is the source of hope for Edwin and Goodchild, represents the new gospel.

The first part of the book begins in an 'inferno', the result of bombing raids in London during the Second World War. The boy, who miraculously walks out of the fire which is 'melting lead and distorting iron' (13), is hideously disfigured with one side of his face darkened, the ear distorted, and the other side normal. His emergence from the fire with a 'ritual gait' into the world, 'his [condensing] out of the shuddering backdrop of the glare' (13), signify the genesis of a being with unusual spiritual power, that becomes increasingly apparent with the unravelling of his pious and dedicated life. His name Matty, short for Matthew '. . . is the device through which several of the novel's themes are wedged, slantingly'.[5] Matthew, who seems to have 'no background but the fire' (17), is a 'gift of god'. Though of this world, he distinctively appears to be of another one, as Pedigree notices, and wonders whether '[he] actually existed when no one else was looking and listening. . . [was] he all connected with everything else or [did] he kind of drift through' (264). That Matty is spirit is implied by his constantly changing last name — Windrave / Windrow / Windgroff / Windy / Wildwave / Winsome / Woodrave / Wildwort / Wheelwright / Wandgrave / Windrop / Windwood / Windgrove / Winddrove. It is the spirit alone which can acquire the qualities of the wind, the ability to be everywhere and to be related to everything. His mission, revealed by his guiding angels and recorded by him in his diary (the gospel of modern times), is the guardianship of a child 'That . . . shall bring the spiritual language into the world and nation shall speak it unto nation' (239).

Matty's unusual spiritual power revealed in the form of his coming out alive from the blazing fire, makes itself felt very early in his life though he is not consciously aware of it. The 'agony of a burning city', having deformed his left side, has made him literal and ugly. Conscious of his repulsive appearance, Matty becomes uncommunicative:

> Because of his hideous face, naïve look, awkward demeanour, and a certain inability to communicate with others there is a primitive grating between Matty and the easy world of his fellows.(53)

While Matty is recuperating in a hospital, adults fail to establish contact with him through words. The nurse who looks after him instinctively knows the "Mattyness of Matty' (18). While 'conceptual artifice' (18) fails to move Matty, it is only the human touch which holds any meaning for him. She can feel Matty comprehending a person's capacity to be at two places at the same time, the duality of human nature. An essentially loving nature brings out immediate response at a show of affection from the young nurse who realizes that 'Matty believes I bring someone with me' (19), an understanding of another dimension, a perception, which increases gradually.

Matty's physical deformity leads to social trauma increasing a sense of loneliness and alienation: 'His limp, his two-toned face and ghastly ear hardly concealed by black hair swept over the baldness of his skull made him a natural butt. This may have contributed to his development of a faculty . . ., which was to increase throughout his life. He could disappear' (22). Matty gets attached to one classics teacher, Mr. Pedigree, at the Foundling School at Greenfield. Mr. Pedigree with his homosexual tendencies, is subject to a 'rhythm' under whose influence the beauty of a child would 'consume him, obsess him, madden him' (22). Living in a world of fantasy, he pretended to himself that he was always the owner of two boys : 'one an example of pure beauty, the other an earthly little man !' (21). While Henderson, 'with his bland and lyric beauty', had the privilege of becoming the first, Matty with his scars and ugliness, was slotted for the latter role. Considering his 'high-mindedness' to be his 'darkest sin', his class-fellows had noticed that his sexuality 'was in direct proportion to his unattractiveness' (22). Basically honest and good with the deep desire to be loved, he believes himself to be Pedigree's favourite when others tell him so. Pedigree's request for information regarding the conduct of class-fellows is assiduously complied with by Matty raising the ire of teachers and students alike. Pedigree, raising Henderson on a pedestal, worships him and is all in all to him. He apparently appears to be exasperated by the latter's repeated visits. Matty's love for Pedigree, his literal-mindedness, and his desire to be good, result in the flinging of his shoe at 'evil' causing Henderson's death and, consequently, Pedigree's arrest. The Biblical curse, muttered under breath, proves by its effect Matty's spiritual powers. Besides having to suffer the revulsion and hate of Mr. Pedigree — 'You horrible, horrible boy ! It's all your fault !' (37) – Matty is constantly haunted by an obsessive sense of guilt and sin for betraying Pedigree, and also, for what he thinks has scarred his spiritual face.

While at Frankley's, Matty's love for Pedigree and his remorse at his own conduct is balanced by his obsessive lust for a pretty girl. 'He had a time that was made of pure, whitehot anguish' (49). Strongly attracted by Miss Aylen, her face, her fragrance, her shinny hair, Matty's mind begins to be occupied by her thoughts as by those of Pedigree. In the author's own words, 'The two compulsions seemed to twist him inside, to lift him up against his own wishes and leave him with no defences and no remedy but simply to endure' (45). While his attempts at communicating his feelings to Mr. Parrish, the van driver, prove futile, his desire to find some consolation in books also seems hopeless. The habitually quiet Matty is repulsed by human speech. Becoming conscious of his own ugliness, he realizes the uselessness of approaching an attractive girl like Miss Aylen romantically. The alternative lay in immersing himself in silence and in forgetting Pedigree's bitter words like 'its all your fault' or the piercing sweetness of Miss Aylen's 'ta'. Suffering at the thought of being unacceptable to a girl, and the impossibility of healing Pedigree, Matty has deeper realization of 'a still dimension of otherness' (48). The existence of a spiritual world, with its appropriateness, truth, and lack of noise impinges on him for the first time. Finding no solace in books 'full of works, physical reduplication of that endless cackle of men' (47), he understands the inevitable necessity for silence, 'the [sinking] down through all noises and all words' (47). For the first time, the resolution necessitates the exercise of his will power, hitherto unused. Looking at the fortune teller's skrying glass at Goodchild's, 'He was aware . . . of a sense of rightness and truth and silence' (48). The meaning of everything is made clear with a light shining into his eyes, unusual, like 'a feeling of waters rising' (48), but illuminating. The conventional methods of the church and prayer fail to bring peace to his disturbed soul. In the silence of the Greenfield church, understanding reveals 'the seamy side, where the connections are' (48), the difference between light and darkness, between beauty and deformity. Once becoming aware of the fact that to approach any girl with his unattractive appearance would result in farce and humiliation, Matty begins to weep tears of understanding. When confronted with the truth, the thought of marriage becomes impossible. The realization of having to renounce this world, for the spiritual one, comes through tears of adult grief. He is, for the first time, faced with the profound questions of his identity and his purpose in this world. Sacrificing all, in penance, he must go out seeking answers to the essential questions. His passionate nature demands that he should go as far away from England as possible. Australia presents itself as the appropriate place for getting an answer to his quest.

The spiritual quest, acquiring intensity in Australia, changes from one of character, 'who am I', to one of nature, 'what am I'. Temptations are in no way lessened by moving out of England to Australia. The ironmongers, rendered dangerous by the presence of a 'girl both pretty and painted' (52) is instantly discarded. The continuous study of the *Bible* cannot bring an answer to the question except to increase perceptions of '... things moving about under the surface' (55). For physical things or things on the surface, there were explicit instructions in the Bible. But for the vague and the indefinable, which remained undeniably deep within oneself, there was no explanation or guidance, a feeling..., which could not be 'defined but [stayed] there, a must without any instructions' (55). Finding no answer to the essential questions at the Sweets' place, where he is employed for quite some time, Matty goes out in search of some other place which would bring an answer to his quest. After a number of jobs he happens to be employed at the houselhold of Mr. Hanrahan which has a room with mirrors fitted on three sides and at the back of the door. Though Matty does not get an answer to his enquiry he sees at the best, his nature on the superficial plane, and the half a dozen different ways in which the world saw him, revealed by the distorted images of his self in the mirrors in Mr., Hanrahan's house, bringing a kind of 'mortification of sinful pride' (59). The sight of Mr. Hanrahan's seven pretty daughters sends him rushing through the wilderness again, asking questions of identity and nature and, eventually, bringing one answer — '*Some have made themselves eunuchs for the sake of the kingdom of God'* (61). The quest for self-knowledge may be fulfilled once he is rendered impotent at the hands of an Aboriginal. Once he is freed from carnal desires, his quest changes from 'what am O' to 'what am I for?' The annihilation of physical desires brings a calm that can rouse deep feelings and the ability to prophesy through signs, like the great prophet Ezekiel, with match boxes, the pot and twigs and the setting of the park on fire. The conflagration hints at the dire consequences in the event of a nuclear test or warfare. While performing the mysterious rituals of going under marshy waters with the weight of chains and wheels on his chest and a lighted lamp held high over his head, in the darkness of night, Matty loses his individuality and becomes 'the man'[. The whole ritual may be suggestive of a passage through the underworld, and rebirth.

Matty feels it necessary to return to England to undo the 'great and terrible sin' (87), and also because of his feeling of being 'at the centre of an important thing' (87). Visited regularly by two spirits, one robed in blue and the other in red, Matty gets an inkling of the path he is to take. Foregoing food, drink, and speech, suffering self-mortification, Matty prepares himself, at the direction of the two spirits, for the great day. On being questioned by Matty about their inability to show themselves everyday, the spirits answer that they disdained looking at his spiritual face which was distorted by his sin. Matty weeps bitter tears when told about his sin which he had already guessed. As he wrote in his journal:

> . . . however ignorant a man is he always knows his sins until he is lost if there can be any like that. Yes it is the terrible wrong I did my dear friend though perhaps I should not call him that he was so high above me, Mr. Pedigree. Indeed , not a day passes but at some time of it I hear what he said to me as they took him away. No wonder my spiritual face dims the light the spirits bring with them, and that lies around them. (93)

The spirits reveal that in spite of the badly scarred spiritual face, he is 'the best material that can be obtained in the circumstances' (93). Contrary to expectations, Judgement does not come on 6/6/66, resulting in dreadful sorrow for 'not being in heaven with judgement all done' (89). But, as the spirits show, 'Judgement is not the simple thing' (101), Matty thinks. In answer to questions of identity, nature, and purpose, he is told that he has something to do with a child born on 6/6/66 with an IQ of 120. On seeing the beautiful Stanhope twins, Matty wrongly assumes that he is meant for them.

Just as the first section of *Darkness Visible* sees the development of good in the person of Matty, the second section sees unequivocal evil developing in the person of Sophy. The two stories develop along parallel lines, though Matty and Sophy progress in two different directions. Matty is an orphan. Sophy's mother is either dead or has abandoned her, and her father is too busy with his chess broadcasts and line of mistresses to give her time. Both Matty and Sophy crave for love but are rejected again and again. From childhood, both witness forces beyond them, operating through them - - the death of Henderson caused by Matty uttering the curse and throwing his gym-shoe, and Sophy killing the dabchick by throwing a stone at it when she is still a child. Matty gets inspiration to follow a spiritual path from the skrying glass. Similarly, Sophy has a sense of weirdness and evil when she feels she has arrested Winnie's soul inside her small transistor. Both are aware of their dual personalities — Matty's two-toned face which shows the good and evil sides of his soul, the two facets of Sophy's personality. Both have a compelling desire to delve deeper and deeper into the working of the forces of good and evil, respectively.

The contrast between the two sections is much more striking than the parallelism. Matty, though outwardly unattractive and foolish, is essentially loving and faithful. Sophy, who is physically attractive and highly intelligent, is, on the other hand, destructive and deadly. Matty is a worshipper of the power of good and light whereas Sophy is dedicated to the power of evil and darkness. Matty voluntarily renounces the world of flesh in favour of the spiritual world whereas Sophy sets out deliberately to get rid of her virginity to fulfil her desire for the weird.

If part I delineates Matty's gradual understanding of the spiritual and mystical world, part II records Sophy's progress from childhood to maturity along with her comprehension of the process of darkness. Sophy becomes the agent of the powers of darkness moving towards destruction and primal chaos with a single-minded purpose. The inevitability of certain actions and incidents, the 'Of course' way in which things sometimes behaved, the occurrence of certain phenomena, 'foreordained from the beginning', become apparent to her with the stone fitting the pre-ordained hand and then moving through the destined arc to kill the dabchick which seemed to co-operate and move inevitably to share its fate with her. The killing of the dabchick with one-in-a-million throw brings satisfaction, and the knowledge of a force working through her and the excitement of imposed will and power also brings the understanding that 'sometimes the arrangement of things is — deliberate' (166).

Sophy's awareness of the darkness within, of its existence in the form of a dark tunnel at the back of her head, and of her sitting at its mouth and looking out into the world, comes before her eleventh birthday, making her shiver, and urging her to escape into daylight. She becomes increasingly conscious of the inner dark being using the outer little girl. The being who was not Sophy but 'This':

> This lived and watched without any feelings at all and brandished or manipulated the Sophy-creature like a complicated doll, a child with all the arts and wiles and deliberate delight-fullness of a quite unselfconscious, . . . a quite innocent, naïve , trusting little girl. (124)

Sophy's cognizance of the 'This' creature brings the revelation of a separate entity which could not belong to anyone, not even to Toni, her twin sister. Belonging was a matter of choice. She could either belong to people by doing what they said was right or choose to follow her own wishes and rules that she knew to be real, dictated by the being at the mouth of the dark tunnel inside her. So, to Sophy, the conventional ideas about right and wrong were not worth much attention and things were right or wrong according to the way one thought about them. Stealing, or stabbing a person were not, in Sophy's consideration, deplorable acts as long as there was an impelling desire to do so.

Sophy's urge to be evil, to be 'Weird', becomes so strong that 'she [finds] herself over come with a passionate desire in the darkness to be weird — there was no other name for it, Weird and powerful' (126). The idea of weirdness, not being clear at this early stage, a floating of the dark tunnel, frightens with its traumatic experience. The first occasion of being weird stems from the impelling desire to hurt her father for his proposed remarriage to Winnie and is satisfied through childish pranks like breaking bad eggs by his bedside and 'aiming the dark part of her head' at Winnie to give her nightmares. Gradually, the feeling of power and imposed will become stronger with the ability to be weird from a distance and, as she assumes, the arrival of uncle Jim from Sidney may have something to do with being weird from afar. That the inside-Sophy is connected with something outside makes itself felt on her hearing two talks in Winnie's transistor which she finds after getting herself rid of her with Toni's help. The talks seemed to speak directly to 'the Sophy-thing that sat inside at the mouth of its private tunnel' (131). The first talk, about the world running down, she feels, she has always known; the other, on experiments in magic and its scientific statistics, had mixed the essence of the dark world connected with 'the other end of the tunnel'. Now she feels that her being would be lost forever, would become an ordinary young girl, if she did not pursue weirdness. It was like an appetite, a taste in the mouth, which 'pushed her, shoved her, craved' (132). This dedication towards evil becomes demanding. Sophy becomes increasingly conscious that one had to 'hunger and thirst' for weirdness with a devotion with which one pursued righteousness.

Sophy's pursuit of weirdness acquires a new dimension of power with the onset of puberty and her coming out into daylight beauty. The dark direction at the back of her head is made all the more distinct and incredible with her realization of a '... desire for the impossibilities of the darkness and the bringing of them into being to disrupt the placid normalities of the daylight world' (134). Sophy now embarks decisively upon the process of exploring the contingencies of evil by setting in motion the disintegration of the world of light. Whereas Matty, in order to reach spiritual heights, renounces the world of the flesh, Sophy gives away her body as a useless, unnecessary, and unregarded thing to any one who wants it. She explores sexuality though, on most occasions, it fails to give her pleasure. On feeling her own turd behind vagina and womb she has convulsions of hate. Sex, at best, is a 'faint ring-shaped pleasure', and orgasm is brought in a sadistic manner through the stabbing of her boyfriend, Roland, with a penknife. The cognizance of evil is like 'the fall of a great arch' (150). There is unwinding, untangling, running down of the darkness within which, finally, joins the force outside leading to complete understanding of evil.

Evil, like good, is a tangle and with clarity of vision Sophy understands that 'The way towards simplicity is through outrage' (167). The final simplicity or unwinding in the form of final victory can be achieved through outrage. Her desire for incest is a kind of outrage which meets with failure. Like the rabbit, flailing about in the trap and killing itself in its efforts to break free, Sophy, too, moves from partner to partner seeking to know the meaning of life. Revelling in a world of sex, violence and power, she hopes to unwind the tangle of her life. Conscious of another dimension, she sees this unfolding as : '. . . the long, long convulsions, the unknotting, the throbbing and disentangling of space and time on, on, on into nothingness . . . .' (167).

Toni Sophy's twin sister, is a foil to Sophy's character. While Sophy dwells deep within herself, examining her inner being, Toni is more concerned with vague intellectual concepts and drifts superficially. Being less emotional than Sophy, she is not much affected by the news of her father's proposed marriage to Winnie, which throws Sophy into fits of crying. While Toni dallys with the concepts of freedom, imperialism, and justice, unable to understand their true meanings, Sophy experiences freedom in its essential form by doing away with social taboos and following her own inclinations. This freedom brings a realization: 'It's the tangle, untangling, sorting itself, slipping and sliding. You must be simple. That's the real thing' (168). Toni, with her smoke — green hair, slim body and a face that could be seen through, has an ephemeral quality which intrigues Sophy:

> It was unfair the way Tony behaved, sometimes , of being miles away, certainly nowhere near her thin body with its empty face; and then proving carelessly, to be present. She would come down out of the air and be inside her head (110-111).

While Sophy has a dark creature sitting at the back of her head, Toni can 'see' through the back of her head easily because there is nothing there. While absorbed in a book, at the Goodchild's, she sees Pedigree stealing children's books with her mind's eye. Not only is she transparent but also hollow inside, being easily affected by other people's ideas. The climax of weirdness is reached with her attempt to abduct a child from a boarding school, through violent methods, with the help of her two lovers. At the thought of this last outrage, a wild glee and fierceness sweep through her. The black sun, symbol of evil, rises with her delirious murdering of the kidnapped boy, in imagination. She imagines that the boy, bound hand and foot, is at her mercy and that she is driving the blade of the knife in her hand into his body, sacrificing him for the power of darkness. By becoming synonymous with evil, she becomes a challenge to the world of light, bringing sin and destruction in its wake.

Darkness is made visible through contrast — good against evil; light against darkness; Matty (purity) against Sophy (sinfulness). The two, developing along parallel lines, move so far apart that the gap becomes unbridgeable till each is each and all alone in this world. The third part, titled 'One is One', brings about a convergence of the various characters, with different points of view, in a world which is multivocal, multiracial and discordant with the sound of screeching jets and growling juggernauts; a world where the forces of good battle with those of evil, the former emerging triumphant in the end. Sim Goodchild the bookseller, Edwin Bell the teacher, Pedigree the pederast, Sophy and Matty, all come in contact with others bringing about a conflict of the powers of darkness and light in the individual and in society.

To Goodchild, the rationalist, mundane matters are of greater importance than 'First Things' (193). Viginia Tiger views him as '. . . an average unbeliever, a skeptic, the novel's representation of ordinary man . . . [resisting] the possibility of authentic religious experience'.6 Living among books, his reactions are conditioned by a conventional literary turn of the mind. The word 'Transcendentalism' triggers off thoughts about the Hindu universe, the great wheel, 'Skandhas and avatars, recession of the galaxies, appearance and illusion –' (200). His beliefs, many and trivial, and mostly acquired from books, do not touch his essential being. Worldly matters such as old family business going to the dogs, the recession of public interest in books, fighting fat and inflation, and his secret longings for the Stanhope girls, occupy his mind more constantly than spiritual matters. On the one hand, the sceptic in him does not readily believe all that he sees and , on the other, another self in him believes in partitions. He believes himself to be a committee of discordant members each separated from the others by impenetrable barriers. Edwin fails to understand what Sim means by being a committee. Sim explains that a single person, sometimes, is an embodiment of many beliefs, 'Different standards of belief. Multiply the number of committee members by the number of standards of belief —' (225). While one of him believes in partitions, the other, oblivious of such barriers, can rise from its bed, go forth, down the stairs, past doors, down the path to the stables that are 'bright and rosy by the light of two small girls' (225). One of them is the 'unruly member' who has a weakness for little girls similar to that of Pedigree's attraction for little boys.

Matty, with his compassionate silence, awakens the spiritual perceptions of the worldly Goodchild who, through the reading of his own palm, is granted revelation:

> The palm was exquisitely beautiful, it was made of light. It was precious and preciously inscribed with a sureness and delicacy beyond art and grounded somewhere else in absolute health . . . Sim stared into the gigantic world of his own palm and saw that it was holy. (231)

Sim experiences the difference between darkness and light, the cosmic and the miraculous, the ridiculous and the pious. Beyond the farcical scratching of the nose there was a word spoken which sounded not like a speech, but music or song. With the desire to scratch his nose, Sim became aware of the existence of two worlds, one narrow and limited, the other wide and spreading beyond limits, 'the one of inches, the other, universal more or less' (232). To remove his hands from the hands of the other members in the séance would mean breaking the small circle. On the other hand, 'if one did detach oneself from the desire to scratch one immediately found how far away those others were, miles, it seemed, so that the circle, instead of being a small one was gigantic, more than a stone circle, county-wide, country-wide — vast' (232). Once the physical desire is satisfied there is concentration on the spiritual and everything seems full of harmony. Speech sounded musical, golden and radiant. It gave indication of the spiritual world which gradually faded from sight but promised to return again. The note from the word spread, 'widened, became . . . precious range after range beyond experience, turning itself into pain and beyond pain, taking pain and pleasure and destroying them, being, becoming' (233). From a time Sim is made aware of devine love which, if asked for, would always return. The ordinary mundane, and somewhat bad man experiences, in Matty's presence, the upward pull of the holy and the good.

Opposed to the loud sounds of the twentieth-century world of jets, trains, and juggernauts, and the tyranny of language, is the world of silence and mystical experience communicated through extra-sensory methods by Matty. This, Edwin believes, can be the only means of attaining salvation. In spite of his enthusiasm for spiritual experience, the impact of the séance, in which he, Sim and Matty participate, fails to touch him as is evident from his misunderstanding Sim's farcical desire to scratch his nose as 'the spiritual combat mirrored in [his] face' (234). Edwin and Sim represent the bulk of the people in this world who are neither good nor bad but something in between. Despite the close proximity of Matty, their spiritual eyes are not opened. While trying to imagine the sublime and the spiritual, they are reminded of the ordinary and the mundane. The room where the séance is held is seen not only as the place for the occult but also as a brothel, with its dust, dirt and stink, and 'the pink lights and bobbled feminity' (247). While trying to perceive the spiritual, Edwin medidates himself to sleep, thereby reducing everything to the ordinary. Trying to imagine some significant spiritual drama which would rescue Pedigree from his hell, Sim's cognizance is that the trouble is with himself. Sim realizes, with a sense of futility, the triteness of the business of living among various categories of beliefs leading on to the 'blank wall of his daily indifference and ignorance' (247), that one is one and all alone and evermore shall be so. On hearing the accusation and laughter of the public during the trial and judgement following the attempted kidnap, and on watching the film of their upper room séance, Sim understands the impossibility of escaping the circumscribed bounds. He also realizes that 'the real public condemnation, was not to be good or bad; either of those had a kind of dignity about them; but to be a fool and to be seen to have been one . .' (255). Refuting the judge's verdict upholding their innocence, he says: 'We're not innocent. We're worse than guilty. We're funny' (258). On hearing Toni cry out about freedom and justice, he realizes the hollowness of the two concepts. The twins, with their youth, beauty, and intelligence, could have lived for more. He himself, and for that matter all the people, could have lived in a more worthwhile manner. As he sorrowfully says, 'A treasure was poured out for them and they turned their back on it. A treasure not just for them but for all of us' (259). Being blinded by his lust for the twins he had ignored the call of the spiritual world. Contrary to Edwin's obtuseness, Sim is perceptive enough to admit his guilt. He may not have anything to do with the kidnapping, 'Nevertheless [he was] guilty. [His] fruitless lust clotted the air and muffled the sounds of the real world' (257); a paradise was forfeited. In spite of this discovery, he does not desist from raising an accusing finger at Pedigree in a final confrontation with him in his shop. He condemns Pedigree for stealing children's books to allure small boys with, ignoring his own placing of children's books at the window to attract the Stanhope twins to satisfy his furtive desire. Althrough Sim is convinced of the hopelessness of the human predicament, of its illusions, delusions, confusions, of the impenetrability of partitions and of each being in solitary confinement, yet he is heartened by the news of Matty's journal which may bring a ray of light into the darkness of his being.

The final battle between good and evil is yet to start, and judgement and salvation are yet to be achieved with Matty becoming a burnt offering to save the child 'that . . . [would] bring the spiritual language into the world . . .' (239), from the fire set on by Sophy's agents. On first seeing Sophy, it was difficult for Matty to decide whether she was good or evil. But observing the signs she showed, he identified her with the whore of Apocalypse. The spirits, attending on him constantly, and supporting him in resisting temptations, show that Sophy had not responded to their call many years back. Throughout the book, evil increasingly concentrates upon Sophy as good upon Matty.

With the augmentation in his spiritual perception, Matty believes that 'What good is not directly breathed into the world by the holy spirit must come down by and through the nature of men' (238). Therefore is his preoccupation with the thought of guarding the boy, and his anguish for healing Pedigree, and his own spiritual face reflected in his maimed, two-sided face. Matty accomplishes the task for which he has been destined, by rushing out of the burning school, himself ablaze from top to toe, to rescue the child the terrorists are about to carry away. The child who is to give the world a sense of direction, is saved, but not before Matty has sacrificed himself for the sake of humanity. Sophy, on the other hand, has been defeated in her purpose with all her plans coming apart. Hysterical rage grips her when she realizes that not only has she been thwarted in her desire to kill a boy but also been abandoned by her lover, Gerry, for her sister Toni. The darkness, which held a sense of cosmic evil for her, now seems empty.

If Matty is the symbol of good then Pedigree, too, has been consistently presented as having a basic innocence of spirit. His dark obsession with the bright sons of morning, the result of his 'rhythm', is his only vice. But he has paid for his sins, and is better than many as he himself says, 'There've been such people in this neighbourhood, such monsters, that girl and her men, Stanhope, Goodchild, Bell even, and his ghastly wife — I'm not like them, bad but not as bad, I never hurt anybody -' (264). Matty loves Pedigree consistently, not only because he has wronged him but also because Matty believes he is capable of being saved.

Pedigree knows the difference between the real thing which we all want, without knowing it, and the 'so many things, . . . sex, money, power, knowledge, the empty things which people consciously strive after'. Understanding that his perversion is a kind of hell, he pleads for help, from Matty, knowing him to be the only person who really loved him. It is only after Matty is dead, and he himself dying, that Pedigree comprehends the former. The park where Pedigree is sitting is filled with sunlight which soaks things in gold and he seems 'to be sitting up to his very eyes in a sea of light' (263). Pedigree is not surprised in the least when Matty 'wade[s] along waist deep in gold' (264), into the park. The quality of the spirit which Matty is, and which his last name signifies, becomes evident to Pedigree as he notices 'the extraordinarily lively nature of this gold, this wind, this wonderful light and warmth that kept Windrove moving rhythmically in order to stay in one place' (264). As the time to free Pedigree from the bondage of his body draws near, Matty is enveloped in gold and his face is no longer two-tone but has a smile round the lips which is loving and terrible. As Matty proceeds to free him, Pedigree resists clutching the multi-coloured ball of his last effort. 'But the hands came in through his. They took the ball as it beat and drew it away so that the strings that bound it to him tore as he screamed. Then it was gone' (265). The working of one's salvation is demonstrated by Matty, who undergoes physical mortification and accepts sacrificial death for the general good. With his intuitive and mystical vision of reality Matty brings light to a world of evil and darkness. Simon, Nathaniel, and Summers, too, with their activities, point out that in spite of the evil in this world there is a Good which is ultimate and absolute. Through Matty, Golding convinces the reader of the presence of a divine grace in this world. The saints guide common men away from a selfish existence to a realization of the supreme will. Blinded by egotism, Pedigree fails to love Matty. But at the fag end of his life he realizes that Matty had loved him all along selflessly and shown a compassion which is beyond human comprehension.

Moving through darkness one is brought to light. Man's volition to escape the limits — what he is and has been, may be complied with at a cry for help. The human pedigree may be cured of its disease and the world become a more habitable place with saintly spirits, like Matty, concerning themselves with man's predicament. As Don Crompton rightly remarks, 'the optimism of *Darkness Visible* consists in its acknowledgement of the possibility of a new order, of saints walking on earth, of a saviour, a new gospel and a new language.'[7]

The use of the Hegelian form of thesis, antithesis, and synthesis, to depict the warring of contrary forces, has made the theme distinct and powerful. The accumulation and the enhancement of the power of good in Matty being the thesis, the opposite, the augmentation of unequivocal evil in Sophy, becomes the antithesis. The synthesis, by bringing about a convergence of the saintly and the sinful, with the former emerging triumphant and revealing the path to salvation, effectively conveys Golding's message of hope in a world increasingly receding towards darkness with man's propensity for evil. The distinctive qualities of darkness and light, as forces active in the world outside and within the individual, are brought home with strength and vigour by contrasting them in two separate parts — Part I and Part II. Part III, revealing the conflict and the co-existence of the two forces, draws the conclusion. The story running along parallel lines, with the similarities and dissimilarities in the lives of Matty and Sophy, in Parts I and II, triangulates itself in Part III, which is a record of the viewpoints of three elderly men: Pedigree, Edwin Bell, and Sim Goodchild. Their lives become connected with Matty's towards the end when they arrange a séance with him. Their perspective joins with that of Matty forming a whole.

The third person narration, at times, becomes obscure with increasing difficulty in following the intentions of the protagonists. The novelist rivets to the first person narration twice in chapter 7 and 14 with Matty recording his thoughts and deeds in a journal, dissipating some of the ambiguity. The supernatural visitations which direct Matty on, in his pursuit and attainment of the good, are recorded here. Frequent use of Biblical allusions, symbols, and encoded clues, while enhancing the metaphysical nature of the tale, also make comprehension difficult. The cryptic, encoded, and telegraphic language is replete with multivocal meaning, and holds constant attention to the intricacies of the spiritual conflict. By acquiring a variety of shades, it brings out the heterogeneity of the complex characters. The intensity of the tale is augmented by the limited number of characters. A steady light is focused on the two major characters, revealing the profundity of their spiritual struggle. The minor characters woven in and out of the tale, add to its texture of perceptions. One is compelled to inhabit the perplexed consciousness of the characters.

The work is complex. Its ingenious construction with narrative codes, opposing points of view, and contradictory perspectives, forces us, as Virginia Tiger has pointed out, 'to accept — at least in the imaginative realm — paradoxes of existence which are to Golding symptoms of the spiritual world.[8]

Unlike Golding's earlier novels, with the exception of *The Spire*, *Darkness Visible* is a hopeful novel, which begins with Matty walking out of the fire, an action which is suggestive of the Apocalypse, and almost ends with his perishing in it. The protagonist suffers the fate of the prophets who warn men in a language that nobody seems capable or desirous of understanding. Matty, by subjecting himself to self-mortification, attempts to purge not only his own sin but the sins of the whole of mankind. That salvation lies not is self-indulgence but in self sacrifice is conveyed through the manner of his death. Man can be redeemed, irrespective of his weaknesses, if he has goodness of heart, as is evident from Pedigree's life. Questions concerning man's nature and purpose, in this world, are thus answered.

NOTES

1. Don Crompton, *A View from the Spire,* Basil Blackwell, 1985, 22-23.
2. Ian Gregor, " he Wondered' : The Religious Imagination of William Golding" *William Golding The Man and his Books: A Tribute on his*

75th Birthday, ed. John Carey, Newyork, Strauss, Girroux, 1986, 93-94.

3. *Op. cit.*, 98.

4. *Op. cit.*, 100 -101.

5. Virginia Tiger, 'William Golding's *Darkness Visible*', *William Golding Revisited*, ed. B.L. Chakoo, Arnold Publishers, 1989, 69.

6. *Ibid.*, 73.

7. *Op. cit.*, 126.

8. *Op. cit.*, 68.

5

Self-absorption of Exoskeletons: *The Paper Men*

The Paper Men, coming after *Darkness Visible* and *Rites of Passage*, the former widely acknowledged as a major novel and the latter enthusiastically received for its concern with the humdrum world, is regarded as a distinctly minor work. Talking about a novelist's practices, Golding has observed that 'a great deal of his work must by the nature of the end product be workaday and pedestrian'.[1] In writing *The Paper Men*, Golding appears to be doing the very thing which Wilfred Barclay, the writer-protagonist of the novel, believed the writer had to do: 'You have to write the bad books if you're going to write the good ones' (108). The novel under discussion concerns itself with the lapses and failures of a self-absorbed writer whose experience of the spiritual being is overwhelming and elusive. He is concerned with some questions regarding the relationship between the artist and the critic, revealing the plight of the papermen in the process. It also delineates the interplay of the superficial and the actual, the symbolic and the literal, what the narrator appears to be and his cognizance of his real nature with attempts to hide it. The most socially realistic of all Golding's novels, *The Paper Men*, while depicting a writer's plight reveals that literature and learning are nothing but paper. Showing the principal characters as two men incapable of much feeling *The Paper Men* questions the nature of the 'social reality' portrayed by fiction in general.

Apparently Wilfred Barclay's running away from Rick Tucker, literary critic, desirous of becoming the former's official biographer, is the central action of the novel. At a deeper level, it is an examination of the metaphysical concept of being which, according to Barclay, is 'the indescribable, inexplicable, the issues, . . . where [one] came in' (116). The metaphor of the two voices of the stream, pointed out to Barclay by the perceptive Tucker, is suggestive of the two levels of meaning:

> The stream, . . . had two voices, not one. There was the cheerful babble, a kind of frivolity as if the thing, the From, enjoyed its bounding passage downward, through space. Then running under that was a deep, meditative hum as if despite the frivolity and surface prattle the thing sounded from some deep secret of the mountain itself. (83)

Barclay, adrift in a world of numinous forces, records experiences of the spiritual world which are direct and bizarre but beyond him to interpret correctly. He admits that the tale, besides being an account of himself and the Tuckers, is 'about more than that, though [he] can't really say what, the words are too weak, . . .' (60). The symbolic and the imaginary often acquire greater importance in a world of perpetual shifting between the mystical and the literal, between the dream and the reality. The reality behind the surface existence, the day-to-day being, is revealed to Barclay by the sound of the stream" 'The deeper voice of the stream had consumed the lighter one. It was as if the mountain was speaking with the same deep tone that had been audible and now, in the mind, visible round the falling lump of rock' (89). The stream brings, too, an awareness of (the earth's unconcern" 'I could feel the indifferent threat of the earth through the soles of my feet, the volcanoes, earthquakes, tsunamis, terrors of nature's fact . . that was what the water spoke of . . .' (89).

Operating on two levels, the novel, while being light superficially, has some metaphysical overtones. On the surface level it is effusive with anti-academic satire. Presenting Professor Tucker as the satiric object, Barclay, the narrator, exposes himself. Though interdependent, the author Barclay and the critic Tucker are always struggling against each other. While a critic's research amounts to searching in the dustbin of the author's life, the author's exposure results in the falling of his trousers revealing his shady past. In their quarrel over paper, they become inhuman and make the people around them suffer. While Tucker's unhandy way of offering his wife to Barclay reveals the slipshod manner of his working, Barclay's inability to accept her is indicative of his weakness. Observing the lack of professionalism in the whole process, Barclay says: 'She didn't know how to do it. But then — I didn't know how to do it! He didn't know how to offer it. Pimp, client and whore, all we three needed the assistance of a professional' (76). Halliday is found to be the man responsible for the whole operation. Tucker, who is merely a representative of Halliday, has been given only seven year's time to complete Barclay's biography. From the mysterious sponsor, whose name cannot be found in *Who's Who in America*, Halliday acquires the stature of a God found standing op top of a church. The 'monstrous Halliday brooding over all' (113) was more dangerous than Rick for 'with his source of information he did not have to guess. He simply knew' (110). Later, Barclay finds himself standing on the roof, near where Halliday had stood, and on looking down, experiences a harmony everywhere. Barclay raises questions about his own identity, of which, as he believes nobody knew except Halliday. Thus there is a deep meditative tone in the narrative. While Halliday appears to be the omnipotent one, Tucker is a sinner tempting Barclay with the body of his wife. With the pin in his hands and feet, Barclay becomes a sort of Christ figure.

Contrasted with the deeper voice is 'the light babbling one', representative of the farce or the low comedy divulged by the account of the relationship between Barclay and Tucker. Tucker rifling in the dustbin for papers, is mistaken for a badger and shot at with a pellet gun by Barclay while his pajama bottoms fell to his ankles. Barclay is uneasily aware of being a victim of the absurd and the inconsistent, of 'the hand of what [he] sometimes thought to be [his] personal nemesis, the spirit of farce' (11). His falling from the precipitous mountain path in Switzerland, and, subsequent rescue by Tucker and his being offered Mary Lou, Tucker's wife, in exchange for giving Tucker the exclusive rights to become his literary executor, are, once again, seen as 'sheer, low comedy all over again' (94). While looking back, each incident in his life becomes an 'added link in some chain of farce, this unbudgeted addition to a whole store of recurrent memories' (90). Though initially it had appeared that Tucker had saved Barclay's life when they had gone for an outing on a precipitous mountain trail, and Barclay, on leaning over the railing, had fallen from the path, yet, later, on returning to this very place, Barclay discovers that, had he been allowed to fall, he would have dropped only a yard onto a flat meadow. Most of the incidents, from Tucker's rifling in the dustbin to his killing Barclay, are farcical. As arranged earlier, Barclay meets Tucker at the Random Club where, as a continuation of the humiliation at Weisswald, Tucker behaves as a dog by sitting on the floor and barking at Barclay, on his arrival. On hearing from Barclay that he was not going to get the much desired permission after all, Tucker, flinging himself on the floor, howls and bites, behaving totally like a dog. Tucker's idea of writing Barclay's biography, too, seems farcical because of the material it would contain. Having cognizance of the great difference between what he appeared to be and what he knew himself to be, Barclay considers his life to be dominated by the spirit of farce. As he admits:

> In one way I could describe my whole life as a movement from one moment of farce to another, farce on one plane or another, nature's comic, her clown with a red nose, ginger hair and trousers always falling down at precisely the wrong moment . . . right from the cradle. The first time I shot over a horses head my fall was broken by a pile of dung. That's farce in good humour. (49)

Barclay and Tucker, the paper men, wandering through a waste-land, devoid of values as informing myths, recall Eliot's hollow men. In writing fiction, money, more than quality, becomes the primary concern for Barclay: 'who cares so long as the money's good? (108). Recognition and promotion, at whose alter wife and self-respect can be sacrificed, become the end for which Tucker pursues scholarship. Barclay, callous and self-absorbed, a product of the twentieth century, is bankrupt both morally and aesthetically. The 'exoskeleton, the carapace', that he appears to be is empty within, with everything eaten away by the worms: '[he] was trapped in [himself] ignorant, bounded by [his] own skin' (114). Alcohol, women, and vice are his obsessions. Tucker, enslaved by his ambition, is unable to protest when treated like a dog by Barclay, and compelled to lap up wine from a saucer. With an awareness of his own weakness, Barclay is convinced of Tucker's feebleness : 'Rick was a paper man. There was no strength in him . . . He wasn't strong or hot or warm' (153). Barclay and Tucker, having lost the connecting link with humanity, have truly become paper men. The former, confessing their moral depravity, remarks: 'Neither of us, critic and author, we knew nothing about people or not enough. We knew about paper, that was all' (76).

Barclay and Tucker, the 'papermen', are each other's nemesis owing to a dearth of love and understanding. Barclay, fixed upon his own sinfulness and self-regard, runs away from God. Just as Pincher Martin, in his self-absorption, had failed to love his well-wisher Nathaniel, Barclay is incapable of loving not only his wife and daughter but also other people around him.

Barclay's habit of collecting every scrap of paper with his writing on it, is consistent with his role as a paper man. Carrying the records of his life, including those of the sordid and shameful events, the scraps bear the incriminating evidence which 'put [him] in danger of losing [his] wife and [his] dignity at the same time' (16). Suffering from a sense of being trapped by paper, it becomes impossible to extricate himself from the heap, to leave it behind, and forget:

> It was as if all paper had become sticky by nature so that whether it was lard or marmalade you could never

> rid yourself of the stuff, once committed to it. It was flypaper and I was the fly. It was the Venus Flytrap, the Sundew, It was those footsteps in the sands of time that I now saw I preferred not to leave behind me. (16)

These lines indicate his realization of the futility and the vulgarity of his pursuits. Withdrawn from humanity at large, the limited association he has with a small number of people, is a result of his being connected with paper, 'from advertising and children's comics all the way through to pornography' (18). The increasing pile of papers, literally flooding the house and giving Elizabeth occasion to nag at her husband, is preserved in tea-chests and cellars. Though the papers had developed into an unnecessary heap, Barclay was possessive about them and was not ready to give them to any one, not even his wife. With misunderstanding growing between himself and his wife, an agreement was reached that she would take the house but the papers would remain his. While at times, as in Italy after a conference, he has no company but the papers, on other occasions they become the cause of his anxiety. Worried about the exposure of the obscene love letters he had written to Margaret, he is, all the same, shocked by the knowledge of her having burnt them. As he says, '. . . in a sky-high pride I had never dreamed that any one could destroy my letters (mad, mad, mad)' (53). The thought that paper can have more value than money at times enrages him. That Tucker offers his wife Mary Lou to him only for paper, humiliates him. In his last scuffle with Tucker, at the Random, there is a literal rain of papers with 'menus, wine lists, bills, order books, bits of manuscripts' (182) flying up into the air and floating like snow. Besides the journals, there are letters to Lucinda and Margaret, photographs taken by Lucinda and Tucker, telephone books or walls or the windows of cars or lavatory paper or hotel menus also carry a record of Barclay's life. On being directed to clear the house of his belongings, after Elizabeth's death, he finds himself in the possession of 'little but the papers' (189). Barclay decides to unburden himself of 'the paperweight of a whole life" (190) in the form of 'unnecessary correspondence, reviews, theses, financial statements, manuscripts, inter-linears, proofs', (190) after recording all the events of his life in his biography and putting the whole lot on fire.

On finding himself the subject of an academic 'light industry' and the target of critics, Barclay intends to revenge himself by writing the book:

> Think Rick — all the people who get lice like you in their hair, all the people spied on, followed, lied about, all the people offered up to the great public — we'll be revenged, Rick, I'll be revenged on the whole lot of them . . .(152).

Golding's ire, too, for the academic 'light industry', by which an author becomes the subject matter, a 'professional meal' (11) for critics, is expressed in his essay, *A Moving Target*. Tucker pursuing Barclay resembles the female post-graduate student about whom Golding wrote in his essay:

> She was not going to write a thesis on anything As dull as a dead man. She wanted fresh blood. She was going out with her critical shotgun to bring home the living. She proposed I should bare my soul, answer all her questions, do all the work, and she would write the thesis on me.[2]

Barclay, the ageing novelist, bears some other superficial similarities with Golding. While the physical resemblance amounts to the 'Yellow-white beard, yellow-white thatch and broken-toothed grin', as an author, his first novel, *Coldharbour,* has been a success like *Lord of the Flies* making him financially secure. They are both inveterate travelers and come from the western part of England. Golding's anti-academic prejudices bear similarity with Barclay's attempt to put off his biographer and critic who makes him the raw materials for his literary activities.

The novel, in general, is concerned with the relationship between the artist and the critic, the author writing and the critic pursuing. On being 'badgered' by Tucker, Barclay is forced to leave his home in England to lead an itinerant life abroad. Tucker, who has the billionaire Halliday to finance his literary endeavours, dogs Barclay's footsteps persistently exasperating him beyond words:

> You've been following me and recording me and pestering me . . . tempting me and persecuting me and buying and selling me all for the purpose of your lout literature. (148)

Tucker, the young American academic, intending to become 'the Barclay man', pursues him over continents, prying into his privacy, recording him, photographing him, and pestering him to be made his literary executor, by virtue of which he would have unlimited access to Barclay's manuscripts, and permission to write his official biography. The temptation to be made immortal through the biography, and as a result a part of the 'Great pageant of English Literature' (44) cannot entice Barclay, for it would mean a revelation of his inglorious and despicable past — lust and perversion with Lucinda, obscenity towards Margaret, disloyalty to Elizabeth, his inferiority as an artist, his plagiarism, and his killing of a South American Indian in a hit and run accident. Observing how an artist and a critic harm each other, Elizabeth remarks: 'You and Rick have destroyed each other' (175). Tucker kills Barclay at the end. As Blake Morrison pointed out, 'Golding is earning himself a place at the butt-end of a literary tradition in which scholars are portrayed as forces of death'.3 The scholar, Tucker, destroyed art in form of the artist, Barclay. Golding writes about his experience of the American academic scene, of how it destroys the artist, 'What a picture of the wild man, the artist destroyed as a kind of human sacrifice, almost a kind of Christ substitute hung on the cross of his own art.'[4] *The Paper Men*, too, exemplifies the idea that criticism at times destroys art.

For the artist, the beauty of his creation lies in its wholeness: on the other hand, a thorough understanding of the work and its relationship with the world at large is achieved through the critic's analysis of work. Barclay's cognizance is of the artist going through experiences like '*mantic* moment, certainties, . . . whole episodes that had blazed, hurt, been suffered for . . .' (25) whereas the critic operated on different beliefs, 'One was that you can *understand* wholeness by tearing it into separate pieces. Another was that there is nothing new. The question to be asked when reading one book is, what other books does it come from?' (25) The critic's work, beginning where the artist's ends, is no less important than that of the latter. Yet, Barclay feels, critics are sometimes oblivious of the painful experiences that the writer goes through. Impatient of critics, Barclay under-estimates their work. The reviewer's pencils are like knives for him. Disdaining to re-read a book just written, he even despises listening to discussions on it. The relationship between Tucker and Barclay is metaphorically illustrative of the essential role of criticism in the form of probing into the depths of a work of art.

The conflict between Barclay, the English author, and Tucker, the American scholar, is suggestive of the danger posed to the living writer by the scholar, perhaps more so by the American scholar. Having toured American universities widely and having been interviewed by American scholars often, Golding may have formed some adverse opinion about them as is evident from his portrayal of Tucker. American billionaires like Halliday, too, do not have good literary taste as they spend money lavishly for biographies on writers like Barclay to be written by scholars like Tucker, the greater part of whose time is spent on pursuing the author over continents and most of the money in paying hotel and conveyance charges. Halliday could influence the academic life of the University of Astrakhan selecting the topic for research according to his own choice, having given them 'the ecumenical temple, the ski jump and the snow machine and the courts for real tennis . . . (66).

Responses to life and reality may be conditioned by extensive reading of literary works. In this respect, Barclay's condition resembles that of the bookseller, in *Darkness Visible* . *The Paper Men* abounds in references and associations: Nabokov (26), Larkin (32, 79, 128), Sheller (32, 79), T.S.Eliot (49), Maupassant (50),

Keats (57, 113), Thomas Wolfe, Hemmingway, Howthorne, Melville (54), Boswell (56, 59), Shakespeare (61, 78, 85, 111, 115, 117), Homer (61), Yeats (68). Johnson (81), Tennyson (86, 89), Conrad (98), Joyce (99), Marlowe (125-6), Beckett (188), At times the associations, used at random, fail to bear any relevance to what the narrator protagonist wishes to say.

Suffering from an artificial passion, Barclay puts very little of himself in his books. Excepting for his first novel, *Coldharbour,* he writes all his other books with less effort and greater economy for which he 'did not need to invent, to dive, suffer, endure that obscurely necessary anguish in the pursuit of the - unreadable' (25). Increasingly recoiling from the world around him and evading involvement, he is compelled to write by manipulating reality. Being an unconscious plagiarist — 'the central idea in my fourth novel was exactly the good one hidden in Prescott's awful manuscript' (111) — and a bad author who writes travel articles and short stories to cheat the public, his only consolation is that one has to write the bad books sometimes. Usually thinking of money, while writing books, Barclay is, all the same, smitten by his conscience for 'scrawling lies on paper' (47). The ordinary and the weak-minded accept these 'lies' as their 'guide, comforter and friend, allegedly, often to their cost' (47). Barclay is beset by doubts about his credibility as a writer on finding Tucker interested in writing his biography.

He is amused by the fact that he should be so mixed up with scholars though his education had finished in the fifth standard. He attributes his success to a specific quality in himself. As he admits, '. . . though you can accuse Wilfred Barclay of being an ignorant sod with little Latin and less Greek, adept in several broken languages and far more deeply read in bad books than good ones, I have a knack' (21).

His inability to love and sympathise with people not only turns him into a morally weak being but also an inferior artist. Once recognized as an important author for his early works, Barclay continues to receive honours and acclaim from the literary world, in spite of writing, subsequently, books of inferior quality. By depicting Barclay in a despicable light, Golding intends, perhaps, to point out the drawbacks of a system which tends to raise writers to a high platform, and accepts everything that they say as the golden words. Their speeches and interviews are regarded as oracles, and are accepted as the means of solving many problems. Barclay is flattered by all the importance given to him. He says:

> I was sometimes called to lecture for my country's good. I did it obediently, at gatherings of academics . . . Academics had to admit that in the last analysis I was what they were about . . . there was nothing in it for me but a bit of flattery, a tiny, perhaps absurd, feeling that my country needed me . . . (21).

Tending to institutionalize such authors the system leaves little scope for self-criticism on the part of the writer. Barclay recognizes the distance between his actual feat and the public acclaim he receives and is haunted by a sense of uneasiness. However reluctant an author may be to yield to the critic and be moved by the literary institution, he is ultimately engulfed and digested by it. All the same, criticism can play a positive role in keeping the writer alert and practicing. As long as he is innovative and creative, the critic pursues him but his attempts to sit or rest results in being swallowed by the critic. Barclay's constant movement makes it impossible for Tucker to harm him but as soon as he pauses, he is killed.

Not only is the author constantly tormented by the critics but is, at times, pestered by the public too. Once involved in the system, however unwilling he may be, the author cannot desist from participating in its norms. In this respect, Golding enumerates his own experience:

> . . . for better or worse my work is now indissolubly wedded to the educational world, I am the raw material of an academic light industry. I should be disingenuous if I pretended not to be flattered and to discount the

> financial benefits which accrue. Nevertheless the situation is not without its drawbacks. The books that have been written about my books have made a statue of me , fixed in one not very decorative gesticulation , a po-faced image too earnest to live with. Nor is this all . A fall-out from my use as educational material means that I get a supply of letters not just from the wider public or from university students but from children as well.[5]

Barclay's resemblance with Golding, to some extent, points to the possibility of *The Paper Men* being a protest against the way writers are treated and the manner in which criticism tends to undermine literature. On the other hand, Barclay's failure to rouse sympathy defeats this purpose to some extent.

Besides being inferior as a writer, Barclay is limited in a more fundamental sense. He is vain, tedious, immoral, cowardly, cruel, and indifferent, even to those nearest to him, as evident from his attitude towards his wife and daughter. His physicality propels him to 'use' the 'shape of a female body' (67). Mary Lou speaks of his, 'liking sex but having no capacity for love' (65). Feeling himself to be a stranger in his own house, his wife's death and his daughter's tears, instead of moving him, make him feel repulsion for them.

Barclay is convinced that the world is a hell where man is constantly damning himself. At times the Good and Evil work hand in hand.

Barclay's intense self-absorption and solipsism fix him in a state of being in which encounters with the divine cannot alter his nature or direction:

> I saw that I had been planned from the beginning. I had my place in things. It didn't matter what I had done or would do. I had been created by that ghastly intolerance in its own image . . . I saw I was one of the, or perhaps the only, predestinate damned. I saw this hotly and clearly. (124)

Understanding himself to be a part of the universal intolerance, Barclay realizes that he could 'only remain integrated by immorality' (17). This leads to the discovery of a being, beyond himself, which is a repetition of his finite self. Though not actively advancing evil, he acquiesces in it, thus becoming all the more dangerous. Holding on to his own sinfulness and self-regard, he can understand his nature to be encased like a hard shelled lobster. The revelation is brought by Johnny, a friend from his London literary days:

> You see, you are what biologists used to call exoskeletal . . . you . . . have spent your life inventing a skeleton on the outside. Like crabs and lobsters. That's terrible, you see , because the works get inside and, . . . they have the place to themselves. So my advice . . . is to get rid of the armour, the exoskeleton, the carapace, before its too late . (114)

The worms of memory, consuming everything inside the lobster shell which is a symbol of determination to isolate and protect one's ego, bring fear of death. Barclay bears close resemblance to Pincher who, for the sake of his overwhelming ego and self-absorption, defies God, and is reduced, on the isolated rock of his being, to two rigid claws. Barclay, conscious of 'what was precious beyond everything' (87), defies death on the mountain and clutches, with all his might, the objects near at hand. Overwhelming ego makes him, not a part of the universe, but, as Elizabeth puts it, 'the whole bloody lot' (173). His uncontrollable ego gives rise to a terrible fear of death which finds expression in a dream in which he sees himself followed by Tucker who chases him in a hearse. Even by taking refuge in a desert , where the ovenhot sand sears the soles of his feet, he finds no relief. The trauma of fear is seen as a 'hole so deep and black it was sickening, like a hole in the universe' (157). While making as assessment of the novel, Don Crompton observes :

> . . . the overall effect of . . . [the book] is to confront an inescapable reality beyond man, a reality whose power

> is fundamentally bound up with the terror of death, the failure to love and the rejection of every thing but the monstrous and furious ego.[6]

While the first half of the novel enumerates Barclay's flight from Tucker, the second half is concerned with his encounter with the numinous, his escape from God. A prey of alcoholism and paranoia, his tale becomes the testament of a 'dipsoschizo'. Barclay's experience of the subliminal makes the narrative open to larger possibilities. Contrary to Pincher's refusal to acknowledge his degeneration and defeat, Barclay, being more of a realist, understands the direction he is taking and admits so to Johnny:

> 'I'm old. I'm going faster and faster-' I think I must have shouted. 'Where we're all going, you Bloody fool!' (116)

Barclay encounters his God, the master of the underworld, in an island which brings up images of hell with its 'powdered pumice with knives of black glass sticking up through it like a feast of steeples' (119), 'its Sicilian burial customs' (120), 'its ancient corpses all dressed up and standing against the wall for support' (119), 'its phosphorescent atmosphere, brassy sea, and smouldering volcano' (120). The cathedral, with its atmosphere 'still darker than it had any right to be, seeing that the sun was brassy outside and most of the windows stark plain . . . a complete absence of gentle Jesus meek and mild' (122) is suggestive of infernal regions. Entering the cathedral, Barclay is confronted by a solid silver statue, with a suggestion of blue, striding forward with red flaming eyes. It could be either Christ or Pluto, the god of the underworld. Barclay is faced with a revelation:

> I knew in one destroying instant that all my adult life I had believed in God and this knowledge was a vision of God. Fright entered the very marrow of my bones. Surrounded , swamped , confounded, all but destroyed, adrift in the universal intolerance, mouth open, screaming, bepissed and beshitten, I knew my maker and I fell down. (123)

His contention with the infernal, resulting in loss of control over his body, brings him cognizance of his being created in the image of the 'ghastly intolerance', of becoming the 'predestinate damned'. A new language is discovered by which 'end' becomes 'sin' and 'sunlight' is 'liquor'. There is an understanding of the fallen state: 'Not. Sin. I am sin' (127), a discovery of divine justice without mercy, Barclay, steeped in his own sin, imagines God in his own image which is akin to Satan's, and the world as hell. The belief that the world is a hell where man damns himself is shared by Golding who has thus observed:

> To be in a world which is a hell, to be of that world and neither to believe in nor guess at anything but that world is not merely hell but the only possible damnation, the act of a man damning himself.[7]

Knowing himself to be damned, and a part of universal intolerance, Barclay understands that he must 'commit afresh' some sin which would become a source of sadistic pleasure. Thus far only acquiescing in temptations, Barclay decides upon committing further evil by torturing Tucker who is likened to 'Johnny's dog':

> I came to the conclusion that the deed most in step with my newly discovered nature would be to kill Johnny's dog. Well. My dog, if you like . . . I saw that a straight forward murder was childish stuff and unworthy of us both, unworthy of image and original what was needed was something philosophically, or rather theologically witty. (129-130)

The 'theologically witty' activity takes the form of humiliating Tucker and lapping up wine from a saucer, by using the permission for his biography as a bait. In the case of his writing the biography, Tucker is made to agree on revealing his offering of Mary Lou first to Barclay and then to Halliday, as mortgage for his continuing academic career. The realization of the state of Barclay's degeneration results in the tightening of the steel string round his chest causing intolerable pain.

That the sinner has the possibility of redemption and is not altogether immune to change is suggested through the next stage of Barclay's spiritual experience. The theologicial change that Barclay undergoes, when shown paradise by Halliday, is very different from the one he experienced in the cathedral, thus exposing the inadequacy of his belief. Barclay, seeing God in the from of Halliday standing on a church roof, is led on to a vision of unsurpassed beauty and unity of being, symbolic of liberation:

> All the people were young and like flowers, I found that he was standing by me on the roof . . . and we went down together and stood among the people with the patterns of jewels and the heaps of flowers all blazing inside and out with the radiance. Then they made music of the steps. They held hands and moved and the movement was music. (160-1)

The transcendent experience, being beyond words, can be expressed only through a metaphor. It is liberating because 'the boil had burst, the pain and the strain had gone' (161), and Barclay, facing the 'assisness, Istigkeit' (161) of life comes to know 'how it is to be human' (161), to be happy. Reality, understood in the form of 'isness', is an involuntary act of awareness. Death, as explained to Elizabeth, is not horrid but 'healthy and right and consonant' (172), the way everybody went.

In spite of this realization, there is no deep change in Barclay. Incapable of any warmth, he realizes: 'We were about as warm hearted as scorpions' (174). His cold and mocking treatment of others is a reflection of the method in which providence worked, making his life a farce. 'Putting aside repetitions, verbals, slang, omissions, it's a fair record of the various times the clown's trousers fell down' (189). The stigmata he received in the hands and the legs may possibly be, as he believed, a sign of his salvation, or another of those farcical incidents to which he is subjected, for being 'a mother-fucking bastard . . . instead of . . . getting them as a prize for being good' (159). When told, by Douglas the vicar, that the stigmata did not necessarily imply salvation, and might, more appropriately, be associated with the crucified thieves than with the Saviour, he feels greatly relieved: 'Not for me the responsibility of goodness, the abject terror of being holy ! For me the peace and security of knowing myself a thief!' (188). An understanding of the theologically witty part of the farce, 'the stigmata awarded for cowardice in the face of the enemy ! (189) cannot dissuade him from hoping for the fifth wound on his side, like Christ, leading on to his salvation. The fifth wound comes, in the form of a bullet hole, from Tucker. Hence he may have the fate of the saved thief.

While on the one hand the novel might be a protest against the threat posed to living writers by academics, on the other, it might be read, as Don Crompton points out, 'as a passionate repudiation of a system that wants to elevate writers to a kind of priesthood.'[8] Barclay may be annihilated by Tucker but he is also pursued by him for all kinds of knowledge about his life, thoughts and beliefs. The insignificant aspects of his work, like the relative clauses in his books, are discussed at length in conferences, revealing the wastefulness of the literature industry which endeavours to collect every possible information on a writer including his follies and foibles.

It is possible to discover in the novel aspects other than that of the writer-critic relationship; it may be viewed as a psychological novel, with regard, in particular, to the exposure of Barclay's evil propensities. We can see his case as that of a moral-degenerate, a person trying to realize himself in an unconventional, un-religious way. Viewed as such, another aspect, namely, the question of sin and redemption, also emerges. The ending of the novel, then, can be called, at the same time, farcical and tragic. The situation that engulfed Barclay and Tucker is the result of their own failure to live upto certain time-tested values like detachment and self-abnegation. They are in that sense the scum of a rootless society, adrift in a world totally dominated by self-interest. The implied moral stand of the novelist then becomes obvious to any sensitive reader.

Autobiographical in form, the novel throws insight into the life of a writer through a phantasmagoric narrative mode. The immediate present, the near past, and the far past intermingle in the text enhancing the dreamlike quality of the narrative. Beginning with the near past, showing Tucker at the dustbin, it ends with the immediate present, the killing of Barclay by Tucker, with the far past coming in between in Chapter V, wherein Barclay remembers the time from childhood upto the time when he saw Tucker at the dustbin. Only on coming to the present, at the end of the narrative, can the meaning of the references to the immediate present, occurring several times in the text (pp. 61, 118, 129, 190-1) be understood. The near past and the present are illuminated through a memory of the far past — his first job as a bank clerk, the discovery of Maupassant, a spell as a groom, the few months as a provincial reporter, going to the war, and the first novel, *Coldharbour*. Chapter V is the heart of the book. It occupies the central position with the chronology of events leading, first from the chapter to the first page, second, to the end of the novel, i.e. the immediate present where Barclay is writing the text. It ends suddenly, without any proper conclusion, because the narrator is shot dead by Tucker, lurking outside the window. The subliminal and psychological condition of Barclay, revealed through this chronology of the events, gives an insight into the condition of paper men. The novel will be remembered as a fine portrayal of the spiritual paralysis that has gripped our times.

NOTES

1. William Golding, 'Belief and Creativity', *A Moving Target,* Faber, London, 1982, 194.
2. *Ibid.* 170.
3. Blake Morrison, 'In Death as in Life', review of *The Paper Men, Times Literary Supplement,* 2 March 1984, 215.
4. *Op. cit.,* 155.
5. *Op. cit.,* 169.
6. Don Crompton, 'The Paper Men', *A View from the Spire,* Basil Blackwell, 1985, 176.
7. *Op. cit.,* 201.
8. *Op. cit.,* 164.

6

Voyage Through the Sea of Reality: *Rites of Passage, Close Quarters,* and *Fire Down Below*

Like Golding's earlier novels revealing his insistent concern with man struggling with the dark forces within himself, either in isolation or in society, the harmoniously structured story of a sea voyage also, presented in the trilogy consisting of *Rites of Passage, Close Quarters* and *Fire Down Below*, reveals a similar preoccupation, though in a spirit of comedy. The voyage, with its storms, tempests, deaths, births, and rejoicing, extending from one end of the earth to the other, is a metaphor for living. Encapsulating a whole society and providing scope for examination of subjects such as moral responsibility, justice, love, neo-Platonic philosophy, rivalry in service, compassion for fellow beings, and uses and abuses of authority, the ship is a microcosm of the wider humanity. While depicting the struggles of the ship and its passengers in diverse weathers — in the equator or the Antarctic— the trilogy unfolds the principal character's gradual progress from self-righteousness and egoism to sympathy and fellow-feeling. While Talbot's growing self-knowledge is the binding theme of the trilogy, the social crisis of our times, made apparent through the stratified world of the ship, is the other important topic under examination.

The trilogy is in the tradition of nineteenth-century fiction and has something in common with Melville's *Billy Budd,* Conrad's *Nigger of the Narcissus,* and Coleridge's *Rime of the Ancient Mariner.* The handling of the nineteenth-century style and narrative frame is deft, plunging the reader into the action of the story with an excitement of event. The story of the voyage is compelling in its clarity and depth. While convincing the reader of the 'reality' of a created world it assures him of Golding's capacity to write in the traditional style.

Comparing the trilogy with Dante's *Divine Comedy,* Stephen Medcalf has observed:

> One might call *Rites of Passage,* where [Talbot] was shaken by Colley's death as he is never quite shaken again, the *Inferno* of the trilogy; *Close Quarters,* where he is first consistently presented as having the grace to feel ashamed and where he meets his Beatrice, the *Purgatorio*; and *Fire Down Below,* where he learns to look at the stars and which is the happiest of Golding's eleven novels, the Paradiso.[1]

Talbot, in this voyage through the living seas of existence, painfully recognizes arrogant pride, sham gentility, conventional hypocrisy and snobbery. The voyage from England to the Antipodes is his initiation — spiritual and geographical — into a totally different world.

The action of the trilogy takes the reader into the early nineteenth century when the Napoleonic wars were coming to an end and the splendour of the Royal Navy beginning to wane. *Rites of Passage,* begun with the serious intention of examining a situation in which 'it was possible for a man to die of shame', had its precise source in Elizabeth Longford's *Life of Wellington*[2] where she describes an episode occurring in 1797. Golding has given an account of the situation in these words:

> There was a man, a parson, who was on board a ship in a convoy that was going from the east coast of India to the Phillipines. They never got there, incidentally, they turned around halfway and came back. But there was a regiment of soldiers going and there was a parson. I'm not sure whether he was, so to speak, an independent parson , a very respectable man. And one day . . . either he got drunk and went wandering naked among the soldiers and sailors, or else he went wandering among the soldiers and sailors and got drunk and naked, put it whatever way . . . But he came back, he went into his cabin and stayed there and no matter what anybody else said to him he just lay there until he died , in a few days and while that story sounds like a sort of old wives' tale, I found that it was necessary for me, for my peace of mind, to invent circumstances in which it was possible for a man to die of shame.[3]

In *Rites of Passage* Golding's enquiry into Colley's death makes the reader constantly aware of a world and its people whose depth can be glimpsed through a dazzling surface. It brings into relief the character of the inmates of the 'wooden world' who have divorced themselves from conscience and whose egotistical pride induces them into self-deception regarding their own vaunted powers. Talbot, who catalyzes the whole sordid sequence of Colley's humiliation, has a slow comprehension of his limited 'knowledge of the springs of human action'. Commenting on Talbot's gradual illumination, Golding says:

> He is learning, you see. He learns very little; he changes very little, but that is the speed at which people learn and change. They don't become great good figures all at once, or great bad figure all at once. They learn their lessons painfully.[4]

The depiction of Talbot's slow transmutation necessitated the writing of the sequels, *Close Quarters* and *Fire Down Below* which, together with *Rites of Passage*, enabled Golding to portray a continuous development in the character. Talbot, who begins as a person conscious of his privileged position in *Rite of Passage,* undergoes a gradual change. Though slow, the change is definite. Talbot, who had disdained to interact with the common sailors and the parson, acquired enough humility, by the end of his voyage, to mingle with the sea men wearing their attire. Man's journey through life is signified by Talbot's journey over the sea to the antipodes. The ship with its numerous characters, represents this complex world. With its hierarchically structured society, the ship is a microcosm of the rigid British class-structure, revealing the social discrimination in which its inhabitants exist. The upper class, comprising officers and gentlemen living in cabins arranged around the mizzen mast, are separated from the common people, — the sailors and the emigrants, . . . living at the front of the ship, by a white line across the deck. Dining with the captain or having a drink with the first lieutenant is the privilege of the upper class which is ever mindful of its position, courtesies, and amorous strategies resembling 'a set of steps in an ancient dance' (57). Summers, when congratulated by Talbot for 'imitating for perfection the manners and speech of a somewhat higher station in life than the one [he] was born to' (125), is bitter about the British class – structure:

> In our country for all her greatness there is one thing she cannot do and that is translate a person wholly out of one class into another. Perfect translation from one language into another is impossible. Class is the British language. (125)

An account of such gradation is given by Golding in his essay 'A Touch of Insomnia' which gives a description of life on a ship:

> The class system was axiomatic. You could not invade a plusher bar simply by readiness to pay more. Nor could you descend to a less comfortable pub if you want to pay less. Where you were born there you stayed. At the beginning — a sort of privilege babyhood — you could glimpse the other worlds. You could pass through doors marked First Class and see the wide bedrooms,

> the stupendous still lifes of sea food on the side tables of the dining room . . . after that the doors were locked. We had to be content with our middle station, right aft, where you got any vibration that was going. And I supposed there was some sealed off hold where the base of our social pyramid rested, where tourists were chained to the kelson under the whips of savage taskmasters, while their flesh was subdued by a diet of weevily biscuits and stale water.[5]

Talbot's cognizance is that contrasted with the people who are higher up in rank and position in society, the ordinary have to be constantly mindful of the infinitesimal gradations and trivial social distinctions. Envious of the people who are above such distinctions, his god father and patron among them, Talbot himself exists, without conscious volition, as the child of privilege. While on the one hand, boundless ambition necessitates climbing the social ladder, insensitive arrogance results from consciousness of social position, on the other. Expressing contempt for people of inferior rank, he distinguishes between Deveral, Cumbershum, and Summers according to birth and education. Deveral is recognized instantly as a gentleman whereas Cumbershum, 'though he sucked in his ale with as nauseating an indifference to polite usage as you would find in a carter' (20), is to be accounted as a gentleman because he held the king's commission. Summers, originally a 'common sailor', had endeavoured to rise from the lower deck to the present position by a process described as 'coming aft through the hawsehole' (51). Parson Colley is specially an object of contempt because he had 'stepped out of his station without any merit to support the elevation', as truth betrayed in every detail of his appearance, manner and speech. That man belongs to an order by nature is Talbot's firm belief. Colley could have been elevated by 'some mistaken quirk or patronage' (67), for his peasant origin is revealed by the lewd songs sung in a state of drunkenness : 'his schooling should have been the open fields, with stone-collecting and bird-scaring, his university the plough.' His alienation is a result of his failure to cope with the social rituals and, as Talbot suspects, due to a lack of 'the natural authority of a gentleman' (106). Being blind to the social reality, he becomes an object of humiliation. On the other hand, status-conscious Talbot achieves a sense of power on perceiving the effect produced by his godfather's name 'among persons of a middle station.'

The story of the voyage is only a way for castigating social snobberies and vices. The satiric intention is apparent as the reader is constantly made to judge what he sees. Sham gentility, class division, arrogance, ignorance, lack of consideration, and irresponsibility are held up to our contempt. The savage brutality, meanness, and malevolence of the 'floating society' (144) are stunning. While the world of the ship involves one with the tragic ignorance, woes, superstitions, and evils of its people, it strikingly reveals the complacence of the English made apparent through Talbot's self-congratulatory attitude. Describing Colley's confrontation with the Captain he says:

> I was moved at this picture in little of one of the elements that have brought English — and dare I say British - - society to the state of perfection it now enjoys. Here before me was the Church; there, <u>aft</u> of me and seated in his cabin was the state in the person of captain Anderson.(106) the ship's society, in short, represents the English society and, as I an Gregor rightly points out, 'It is not difficult to infer that the name of the ship is *Britannia*'.[6]

The action in the ship, ' a floating theatre', is dramatic. As Golding says, 'It had to be theatrical because [Colley] had to make an exhibition of himself, and therefore the ship had to be turned into a theatre in which he could do it. So in that sense, it is a dramatic story, a dramatic performance.'[7] the ship, being a convenient metaphor for the theatre, becomes a place where people exhibit themselves while undergoing a sea-change — Captain Anderson, Edmund Talbot, Mr. and Mrs. Prettiman, and those employed in the ship. The deck becomes the main stage having two side-doors opening out on it from the forecastle. The quarterdeck, housing the higher class passengers, represents the galleries with a view of the action on the inner stage. The plot, spread over a trilogy, follows a three act division with the main theme being Talbot's education. Act I, introducing most of the characters and the general situation in *Rites of Passage*, presents the mystery of Colley's vision, humiliation, and remorse along with Talbot's gradual comprehension of his own shortcomings as a social being. Act II shows Talbot falling in love with Marion Chumley from another ship, the crippling of the ship by the folly of an officer and a midshipman, the gaining of a better officer, Lieutenant Benet, and the monstrous suicide of Talbot's servant, Wheeler - - all these taking place in *Close Quarters*. The climax is reached in Act III, in *Fire Down Below*, with the ship's danger increasing as it reaches the Antarctic. Tension grows between Summer and Benet as the latter tries to save the ship using ingenuous methods. The painful memories of Colley, Wheeler, and Marion Chumley become unbearable to Talbot. The kind-hearted Summers helps him face this emotional crisis. The denouement is reached with the ship arriving safely in Australia and Talbot joining his work and meeting Marion Chumley once again, almost by chance.

Talbot endeavours to explain the nature of the drama through his journal using metaphors from the theatre. His encounter with Zenobia, the ship's doxie, is related in dramatic terms: 'We were to perform. But before act one could be said to be well under way . . . louder exclamations from Mr. Prettiman and louder rumbles and even thunders from Mr. Brocklebank turned her to seriousness again.' (58) His seduction and the 'boarding' of Zenobia are described thus "'We were now . . . in about act three of an inferior drama. She was to be the deserted victim and I the heartless villain' (88). The whole episode with Zenobia is seen as being 'borne along on a tide of melodrama' (99). Colley's exhibitionism in a drunken state takes the 'shape and dimensions' (115) of a drama with the forecastle as the stage and all the inmates of the ship collecting on the afterdeck and the quarterdeck, as spectators. Captain Anderson, encouraging Colley's humiliation resulting in his death, is the villain of the latter's drama. The play put on by the passengers for the entertainment of the lower classes becomes a play within a larger play.

The glimpse of Colley received from Talbot's journal is reversed by the one got from Colley's letter. Presenting the romantic effusions of the writer, it makes one see the incidents of the early part of Talbot's journey in a new light. Talbot presents him as an ugly social misfit : 'Surely his frame was not one that could afford him any pleasure. His skill was seen to be small and narrow. His legs had no calves; but dame Nature in a frivolous mood had furnished him with great feet and knots of knees that betrayed their peasant origin' (117). Contrasted with this picture is the one of a man essentially innocent, sensitive, and religious:

> I tell my self that OUR LORD is here as Much as there; or rather that here and There may be the same place in HIS EYES. (190)

Again,

> What has remained with me apart from a lively memory of my apprehensions is not only a sense of HIS AWFULNESS and a sense of the majesty of HIS creation. It is a sense of the splendour of our vessel rather than her triviality and minuteness. It is as if I think of her as a separate world , a universe in little in which we must pass our lives and receive our reward or punishment . . . . It is with me still for, the breeze dying away, I ventured forth again . . . . I remained motionless by the rail . . . . While I was yet there, the last disturbance left by the breeze passed away so that the glitter , that image of the starry heavens, gave place to a flatness and blackness , a nothing. All was mystery. (191-192)

For the devout Colley the whole voyage is a spiritual one, revealing the power and the glory of God. He watches with awe the heavenly spheres: 'On her right hand the red sun was setting and on her left the full moon was rising . . . The two vast luminaries seemed to stare at each other and each to modify the other's light . . . . Here plainly to be seen were the very scales of GOD' (233). Love of God prompts a love for all objects and human beings. In spite of the terrible humiliation inflicted on him, he can forgive them in the true Christian spirit.

Colley, deeply emotional, is basically simple, lacking the worldly cunning necessary to face ruthless, arrogant and despotic people like Anderson. Judging things more by feeling than by a practical sense, he fails to see the world as it is. Ignorant of the snobberies of a stratified society, where people of the higher station consider it necessary to express contempt for people of inferior rank, Colley finds himself increasingly left out from the social world of the quarterdeck. He lacks insight, and is a bad judge of his fellow-men. Thus Talbot is seen as a true gentleman: 'He is a member of the aristocracy, with all the consideration and nobility of bearing that such birth implies' (194).

Colley is faced with his own weaknesses. A sense of guilt and sin is heightened when he becomes aware of his attraction for the young and handsome Billy Rogers. Added to this is the humiliation inflicted by the ship's vulgar society.

It is customary among the inmates of a ship to observe a rite while the ship crosses the Equator. The rite consists in throwing some passengers into a pool of dirty water while Neptune sits in judgement. A parson who is supposed to bring ill luck to a ship, is considered the most suitable person for the immersion. While the whole incident amounted to innocent fun for the sailors and the passengers, for Colley it symbolized God's judgement. He felt that Nature herself was a witness of the fact:

> On [the ship's] right hand the red sun was setting and on her left the full moon was rising , the one directly across from the other. The two vast luminaries seemed to stare at each other and each to modify the other's light . . . . Here plainly to be seen were the very scales of GOD . . . . in that vast ship with her numberless

> souls I was alone in a place where on a sudden I feared the justice of GOD unmitigated by HIS mercy ! On a sudden I dreaded both GOD and man ! (233-234)

Sensitive by nature, Colley views the shortcomings in his character as the source of all the trouble.

Looking at his omissions and imperfections as sins he holds certain incidents responsible for bringing him to this day of judgement. Though aware of the captain's hatred of parsons, Colley holds himself responsible for the former's anger at seeing him. Failing to notice or read the captain's orders, prohibiting all passengers to enter his quarters, Colley goes to meet him and is snubbed vehemently. As a clergyman his failure to hold regular Sunday services for the passengers or appear in the appropriate attire before them are considered by him to be sins against the Church. Added to this is his weakness for the handsome Billy Rogers. By subduing his personal feelings he had planned to convert Billy Rogers to the Anglican faith. In this, too, he fails. Not committing any serious crime, he believes himself condemned and is ready to accept Neptune's judgement. Carried by Cumbershum and Deveral, Colley is thrust into the badger bag filled with sea water, dung and urine. Repeated protests fail to rouse their sympathy:

> As I opened my mouth to protest, it was at once filled with such nauseous stuff I gag and am like to vomit remembering it. For some time . . . this operation was repeated; and when I would not open my mouth the stuff was smeared over my fac e . . . each question was greeted with a storm of cheering and that terrible British sound which ever daunted the foe : and then it came to me, was forced in upon my soul the awful truth – I was the foe ! (237)

This cruelty brings the realization that 'nothing that men can do to each other can be compared with that snarling, lustful, storming appetite . .' (238) which is worse than death. Shame burns him, yet there is solace that it has been inflicted: 'What a man does defiles him, not what is done by others' (235). It is when Colley awakens to his unconscious infatuation for the deckhand and discovers the guilt and sin at the centre of his being that he wills himself to death. His anguish is described by Talbot:

> It was then I perceived without seeing — I know, but had no real means of knowing — There had been a time when he had awakened in physical anguish which had quickly passed into a mental one. He lay like that in deepening pain, deepening consciousness, widening memory , his whole being turning more and more from the world till he could desire nothing but death. (156)

Uniting the sensual and the spiritual becomes impossible for Colley. Unable to face the darkness and chaos within his self, he sinks into despair and ends his life. His story eludes total explanation, suggesting the incomprehensibility and mystery of certain things in life. A truth which makes Talbot exclaim: ' Life is a formless business . . . Literature is much amiss in forcing a form on it'. (265)

Apart from being sensitive, Colley is egocentric, using his religion to hitch 'himself up a little bit in the pyramid beyond his origins'. 8 His egoism takes the form of religious fervour. Naively he believes that he can elicit respect from fellow-passengers and sailors by donning his priestly finery, thereby projecting the image of some sort of authority. His firm belief is that 'a clergyman without his bands and wig would be of no more account than a beggar' (225). Therefore he does not want anybody to mistake his sanctified identity' (224). He is careful not to be seen without his 'uniform'. According to Colley the people of the ship had demeaned God by insulting him and he considers it his duty to rebuke them. As he says:

> There remains the insult offered not to me, but through me to ONE whose NAME is often in their mouths though seldom, I fear, in their thoughts ! The true insult is to my cloth and through it to the Great Army of which I am the last and littlest soldier. MY MASTER

> HIMSELF has been insulted and though HE may - - as I am persuaded HE will forgive it, I HAVE A DUTY to deliver a rebuke rather than suffer that in silence ! (240-241)

Dressed in his hood, square, bands, wig and hat and carrying his license in the tail-pocket of his coat, he confronts the Captain who mumbles a confession. Assuming a superior air he tells Captain Anderson : 'after this confession of your fault I forgive you freely . . . I defend MY MASTER'S honour as you would defend the king's' (242-243). When the realization dawns that the *cloth could not bring* the much desired respect, life becomes a burden for Colley. Golding says : 'The terrible thing for Colley would be to fall below that; and of course he does, with a crash. And that is the end of him.'[9]

Neither in life nor in death is Colley to have peace. The cannon balls, fastened to his feet to pull his body down to the depths of the sea, of which he had been afraid, signify that the continuing torment, begun on board ship, must continue after death.

While Colley is motivated by a selfless love for human beings, Talbot has a view of life firmly based on man and his institutions and is found to be utterly class-bound, fastidious, and complacent at the beginning of the voyage. Incapable of glimpsing into the depths of a character's being, he fails to sympathize with Colley or understand the significance of his experience. That his judgement of men and women is inadequate is apparent from his summary assessment of the characters of Anderson, Deveral, and Summers. Believing too much in the importance of his position, Talbot is confident of his ability to manipulate the captain and consequently other matters in the ship. The captain is seen as a tyrant and the persecutor of Colley. Much later, when the truth of the captain's birth is revealed by Deveral, Talbot realizes that the captain has been the victim of social pride and prejudice. Summers, who is seen as a common sailor, elevated to the position of a lieutenant through his own efforts, is congratulated for imitating the manners of a higher station, while Deveral is considered to be a true gentlemen. Talbot's opinions are reversed with the discovery of Colley's letter to his sister which reveals Deveral's positive part in victimizing Colley. Thus, far from being an ornament to the service, Deveral was a disgrace to a noble family. It was Summers, with his compassion, sense of justice, and fair play, who did credit to 'His Majesty's Service'. Colley's letter, which serves as an eye-opener, also reveals that his attitude towards Talbot is one of genuine love and esteem while he is mistaken for a sycophant. From the various events, Talbot realizes that his knowledge of human beings is limited. For him the end of the first part of the voyage brings this realization: 'With lack of sleep and too much understanding I grow a little crazy. I think, like all men at sea who live too close to each other and too close thereby to all that is monstrous under the sun and moon'. (278)

While Talbot's insensitivity and partial insularity can be excused, Brocklebank's obtuseness, in spite of the fact that he is an artist by profession, points to the failure of some artist to grasp certain realities of life with a subtlety expected of them. Juxtaposing Colley against Brocklebank, it is effectively pointed out that not all artists are as sensitive as required to be. Colley, though a parson by profession, is over-impression-able, perceptive, and responsive, while Brocklebank is blunt and thick-skinned and oblivious to a number of things, revealing that sometimes artists too can remain untouched by the human predicament that surrounds them. Dealing with art can, at times, distance the artist from actuality. Though Brocklebank is prompted by the thought that 'there is more profit in the Muse than in the other thing' (168) to take up art as a profession, he prefers to keep reality and bitter truth at arm's length. That an artist cannot afford to confuse art with actuality is evident from his painting of the death of Nelson. Though the painting depicts Nelson dying, surrounded by mourning and grief-stricken sailors, in actuality he must have died '. . . down below in some stinking part of the bilges . . . with nothing to see him by but a ship's lantern' (169), often the artist is prompted by monetary considerations to portray scenes removed from reality. Perhaps a desire to run away from reality prompts artists like Brocklebank and Barclay to become 'dipso schizo'. Indulging in wine and women, he is often in a state of drunkenness and on looking at the dead Colley fails to ascertain whether he is dead or alive. He says, 'I know you all . . . I am an artist! The man is not dead but shleepeth ! He is in a low fever and may be recovered by drink . .' (177). Here, too, is an attempt to hold reality at arm's length.

While the rites of crossing the line were observed without emotional involvement, and in dramatic terms, attention now shifts from the public to the private and intimate, where feeling is no longer only observed but personally experienced and registered in *Close Quarters*. Talbot, after racking his brain for a hero, decides that

> [he] should perhaps tell the story of a young gentleman of much intelligence and more feeling than he was aware of who takes a voyage to the Antipodes where he is to assist the governor of the new Colony with his undoubted talents for something or other.[10]

Talbot's transition from the classically Augustan man of thought to a romantic person is the chief interest of *Close Quarters*. Moved by the events surrounding Colley's death, Talbot becomes aware of the extent to which a man can despair of this surroundings and sink into abysmal depths of hopelessness. Becoming conscious of the inherent cruelty and unfairness of life, Talbot begins to see things at close quarters, learning a great deal in the process. He begins with certain beliefs about the importance of the civilized nations who would, according to him, increasingly take over 'the administration of the backward parts of the world' (9). According to him, the British excelled in the world because of the 'true genius of [their] system' (10). Belonging to the eighteenth century British aristocracy he opines that only a chosen few should be eligible to form a government. He says:

> The more civilized a country is, the smaller is the number of people fitted to understand the complexities of its society. A civilized community will always find

> ways of healthfully limiting the electorate to a body of highly born , highly educated , sophisticated professional and hereditary electors who come from a level of society which was born to govern, expects to govern, and will always do so. (11)

The inadequacy of his beliefs is revealed with Deveral, belonging to a family 'born to govern', proving himself callous, irresponsible and negligent towards his duty. Requiring to drink wine before carrying out his duties, he makes a fiasco of his work and literally becomes that Devil as his name signifies. Though entrusted with the charge of the ship, he leaves the deck for a drink, asking Mr. Willis, a mere mid-shipman, to keep watch. Young and inexperienced, Willis fails to take the right action when a sudden gust of wind catches the wrong side of the sails. Through his carelessness, Deveral contrives to strip the ship of its sails, thus making the 'floating society' vulnerable to a painful, troublesome, and dangerous journey. Talbot's thoughts and convictions change gradually, the transformation being initiated with his metaphorically receiving a 'blow with the flying sheet' (39) first and then accidentally striking his head on 'the deck so concussively that the whole world was obscured for a moment by a brilliant display of lights' (43).

Talbot's change, from a calculating and reasoning person to a 'Man of Feeling', is initiated by his falling in love with Marion Chumley. His first meeting and its overpowering effect is described in the following way:

> The lightning that struck the top of the mizzenmast ran down, and melted the conductor into white hot drops. The mast split and flinders shot every way into the mist. The deckhead burst open and the electrical fluid destroyed me. It surrounded the girl who stood before me with a white line of light. (87)

His love, bordering on sentimentality, while turning him into a poet, tends to make him forget his single-minded ambition. Talbot tends to experience love through prior literary texts such as Homer,

Shakespeare, Virgil, Byron, Pope, and Dryden. All the books read earlier, *The World Well Lost* or *All for Love* to some extent, seemed to echo his overwhelming passion. For him Marion becomes the sum of all the poetry he had read. As he says:

> Oh, *thou,* Marion, rising from the meekest and deepest of curtsies, sum of all music, all poetry, distracted scraps of which with their newly irradiated meaning tumbled through my mind ! (CQ 88)

Undergoing a drastic change from a Man of Reason to a Man of Feeling, he cannot help exclaiming, 'what a translation was there !' (106). Constantly making him think, burn, and pine for Marion, his love, while making him delirious and oblivious of worldly affairs, subdues everything in him, making him wish to immerse himself in the sweetness of his enchantment and overthrow.

Delirious from a delayed concussion, Talbot goes through experiences which, while being strangely reminiscent of Colley, give Talbot a 'complete understanding of one's situation' (134). Just as Colley, when forced to drink wine, had made an exhibition of himself, singing loudly in front of the people of the whole ship, Talbot, too, when given the paregoric, falls asleep, singing and weeping, on Colley's bunk. While Colley had woken up to his shame, Talbot woke to realize his loss with the disappearance of *Alcyone* across the horizon, carrying his beloved Marion Chumley. When attempting to call back the *Alcyone* by climbing the sails, Talbot is forced back into Colley's cabin and has the door locked on him from the outside.

Though pining for Marion, and heedless of the affairs of the ship for a number of days, Talbot is forced to bring himself back to practical matters, owing to the precarious condition of the ship. Moving from the narrow units of egotism and self-concern to a wider consciousness of people and problems around him, Talbot, for the first time, begins to have contact with people in the lower parts of the ship. Though he had visited the 'nether regions' of the ship earlier, he hadn't understood the people there as well as he did in his later visit. As he admits:

> Now that I was descending again through those shadowy, those heaving and creaking and dripping and trickling levels, I understood only too well the difference between that descent and this one (156).

Discerning Talbot's growing altruism, Summers exclaims, 'At moments I even detect a strong streak of humanity in you as if you was a common fellow like the rest of us'. (178)

Talbot's growing fellow-feeling brings about his unconscious identification with Colley. A complete understanding of Colley's shame and death necessitates Talbot's moving into Colley's former cabin and his sleeping on the very bed on which the man died. Constantly thinking of Colley, Talbot plays the former's role in a dream sequence. Appearing 'unclothed' before the laughing people of the two ships, he merges with a woman who 'was there on the deck, her arms outstretched. Tears of joy streamed down her cheeks' (222). Comprehension of Colley's condition gives birth to a new self in Talbot.

That human nature eludes total explanation is metaphorically presented through Talbot's encounter with the 'awful creature which was rising from the unknown regions' (257). Recognizing partial responsibility for Colley's death, Talbot is faced with the dark part of his nature in nightmares where he encounters the awesome and dreadful creature. The awful thing is experienced both by the dreaming and the waking self and is described in the following manner:

> My dreaming spirit fears as my waking spirit fears that one night the thing will emerge , bringing with it a load of weed that only half conceals a face . . . I saw with waking eyes down by the crazily unstable waterline something like the crown of a head pushing up through the weed. It was a head or a fist or the forearm of something vast as leviathan. (257)

Resembling Jocelin's confrontation with the dark depths of the pit or Matty's walking through the waters in a dark forest or Sammy Mountjoy's nightmares in a cellar, Talbot's experience signifies an encounter with the fundamentally unknowable in the self. Having a glimpse of the mysterious, Talbot is awed by a vision of cosmic disorder. For him the appearance of the inscrutable objects 'cancelled the insecure 'facts' of the deep sea and seemed to illustrate instead the horribly unknown' (257). Life seemed to be a feast of experiences with all the courses served in quick succession. Not operating in a reasonable fashion, it evades comprehension. Eluding total explanation is the mysterious suicide of Wheeler in Talbot's cabin. Wheeler talking of being in hell and having convulsions on hearing of devils, is an enigma for Talbot. His self-immolation defies all logic and is beyond Talbot's comprehension : 'I have tried again and again to put what I saw in logical order but come always to the fact that there was no order but only instantaneity' (262).

Talbot's progression from insularity to a gradual and sympathetic understanding of people is signified metaphorically by the disappearance of the white dividing line which had been drawn across the deck at the mainmast and by his willingness to keep people's messages in his firkin. Joining hands with Summers in a gesture of friendship, Talbot admits: 'I am learning too much, that is the fact of the matter. Men and women . . . . . I had proposed myself a political and detached observation of the nature of both' (269). His association with Summers, Marion Chumley, and Wheeler, forces him into public space. Interaction with people brings about an understanding of his own self.

Fire Down Below, the third novel in the trilogy, along with moments of tension, insight, and humour, is encompassed in mystic suggestions. While the earlier two novels had examined man's position in relation to his fellow beings, the third novel attempts to ascertain his place in the universe, his position in relation to the sun, the moon, and the stars. On looking at the spheres in the sky, one cannot help wondering about the creator, who may be variously called God, as by Summers, or 'the Absolute' as Prettiman viewed him.

On the literal level, the title signifies the fire left smouldering below the deck, at the time of the heating of the metal shoe holding the foot of the mast, while the red-hot-iron support bolts were being driven deep into the wooden structure of the ship. This fire, smouldering silently below the deck, bursts into violent flames consuming the ship, a microcosm of the bigger world, towards the end of the long voyage.

Throughout the novel, Summers and Benet try to ascertain the position of their ship in the vast ocean, with the help of the longitude and the stars. It is symbolic of man's endeavours to find his place in the universe, both physical and spiritual. Prettiman's mystical view of man's position is juxtaposed against Summer's orthodox Christian belief that 'No man can contemplate it without being put in mind of his Maker' (90). Man's search for direction is answered once he is successful in ascertaining his position in the cosmos. While Summers and Benet are engaged in finding their position on the globe, Prettiman is concerned with finding man's place in the universe. As he tells Talbot, 'what could be better than ascending from the trivial matter of our exact position on this globe to a contemplation of the universe into which we have been born?' (218)

Fire Down Below, sees the final stage in the making of Talbot's character. What is seen as transformation in the other passengers by Talbot is in fact owing to a change in his own self. As he says: 'during the increasing decrepitude of our ship and more evident danger to our lives, there had been a corresponding change in the character of the passengers and change in the relationship between us' (30). The change from customary clothes to a sailor's uniform while signifying an increased fellow-feeling is also indicative of Talbot's decreasing sense of self-importance. The sadness of self-knowledge brings an understanding of the shortcomings of his character while he recognizes his part in Colley's and Wheeler's death and admits that he could have saved them. Added to this is the probable death or Prettiman, on his conscience, which was like 'falling into the darkness of a measureless pit' (145). Sustaining him through this emotional crisis, Summer's friendship and Talbot's esteem for him are the only ray of light in a sea of darkness. As Mrs. Prettiman puts it, '. . . at moments when your careless assumptions of privilege have been most provoking you have been rendered tolerable by your evident admiration for that worthy man' (196).

After having known from Summers what true friendship is, Talbot is led from the trivialities of this world to contemplation of the universe and the Absolute by the social philosopher and inspired visionary, Mr. Perttiman. persuading Talbot to recognize the beauty of the universe and our place in it, Prettiman says:

> Imagine our caravan, we, a fire down below here . . sparks of the Absolute — matching the fire up there . . out there ! Moving by cool night through the deserts of this new land towards Eldorado with nothing between our eyes and the Absolute , our ears and that music ! (219)

Though momentarily drawn by the power of Prettiman's vision and glimpsing the universe 'as a bubble afloat in the incommensurable golden sea of the Absolute' (220), Talbot is disinclined to embrace Prettiman's mode of thought and living, in place of the conventional. Unwilling to make sacrifices necessary for setting up an idyllic world, Talbot chooses to take refuge in the formulaic:

> I saw already that the price was impossibly high. I am after all a political animal with my spark . . . I suppose the excuse to be presented to the Absolute is that I did and do sincerely wish to exercise power for the betterment of my country: which of course, and fortunately in the case of England, is for the benefit of the world in general. (221)

By rejecting Utopia for the exercise of political power, Talbot proves himself to be the average man for whom 'the Absolute' remains a dream. Tied down by worldly considerations, Talbot cannot think of aspiring as high as the Prettimans, as is signified by his dream about them, revealing his attitude to life. He records of this dream at the end of his journal:

> That night I had a kind of dream. I hope it was a dream, for dreams in any event are mysterious enough. I do not mean their content but the very fact of them. I do not wish it to have been more than a dream: because if it was, then I have to start all over again in a universe quite unlike the one which is my sanity and security... I was seeing them from ground level because I was quite comfortably buried in the earth of Australia, all except my head. They rode past me a few yards away... laughing and chattering... with faces glowing as in a successful hunt for treasure . (312)

Talbot , disinclined to re-form and re-shape his aspirations, prefers not to hazard his social security though he is attracted by Prettiman's vision and the possibility of a better world.

Though Anderson is seen as a destructive and malicious egotist by Colley, the Prettimans have no doubt about his ability as a good Captain. Cool headed and firm at the time of crises, Anderson is described by Mrs. Prettiman as 'our grim captain, the right man to get us where we are going' (193). Commenting on him in an interview, Golding has said:

> He is unjust to Colley, it's perfectly true, therefore he is a tyrant in that sense. He is a captain of a ship, which means he must have absolute control... There are people like Summers, there is Miss Granham, and there is the sociological gentleman, Prettiman. There are a number of people about the place who would pass muster in society as being on the plus side o f things, and then there are lots of people who are just people the way most people are just people — the gunner, the carpenter, the sailing master. Well, one of the lieutenants is pretty much of a slob, but the others are

> all right. And Anderson would be a good sailor, a good captain. He might be a stern Captain, but then in those days Captains had to be stern. The ship has fools on it and follies are committed.[11]

Capable of recognizing a man's wroth, Anderson permits Benet, is spite of Summer's vehement protests, to apply his ingenious and innovative methods in saving the ship. Though Summers is rebuked for becoming an obstruction in the way of progress, he is all the same recommended for captaincy by Anderson. Benet, a competent seaman, brilliant technician, poet, lover, and romanticist all rolled into one, is the opposite of Summers who, adhering to the old system, is afraid to risk any technical innovation in the matter of the ship. While tension grows between Benet and Summers the former's ingenuity saves the ship from being wrecked. The two strands of romanticism and realism run side by side in his character. Benet is a maturer lover than Talbot. Looking at Talbot's infatuation for the young and immature Marion Chumley with disdain, Benet himself is enamoured of a woman much older than himself. On the other hand, Summers, with his sturdy sense of loyalty and dedication to duty, helps Talbot pass through the critical moments of his voyage. His intuitive kindness enables Talbot to face the memories of Colley and Wheeler in the very cabin where they kill themselves. Incapable of aiming very high, he is satisfied with his promotion to the position of a midshipman first, and the captaincy of a ship of line, later.

Pursuing an idyllic world which defied the traditional political, social, and linguistic demarcations, the Prettimans are an ideal couple. Without any thought of personal gain they love each other selflessly. Once committed to marrying Mr. Prettiman, Miss Granham does not desist from doing so even after finding him almost a dying man. A crisis prompts each to be more concerned about the other's welfare. On finding that the ship could be sunk by the iceberg, Prettiman tries to persuade Talbot to take Mrs. Prettiman upon deck, leaving him in the cabin, so that she might stand a chance of survival. Unable to contemplate separation from her husband, she refuses to leave him. Attached to him not because of material consideration but for the visionary that he is, she tells him: 'In the short span of our married life I have never disobeyed you and would not have done so in the future had there been one, not because I am your wife but because of who and what you are!, (238). Dressing herself in the practical clothes of a seaman, and wearing trousers and riding astride (unusual for a woman of the nineteenth-century), Mrs. Prettiman compensates for her husband's disability by doing the work he is unable to do.

Throughout the novel there are indications that appearances may be deceptive and things cannot be judged by what they seem to be. Talbot is momentarily deceived into mistaking the brightness of ice as day break. The apparent antagonism displayed by captain Anderson and Benet towards Summers, during the voyage, proves unsubstantial when they both recommended him for promotion to the position of captain (268). What appeared to be Benet's effusions of love for lady Somerset was only his attempt to recite poetry to her while being accidentally thrown on her by the ship's movement (300). This results in Benets removal from *Alcyone*. The dichotomy between what one believes to be the truth and the actual truth is made apparent by exposing the basis of such belief as illusory.

The memory of Colley haunts the ship and its inmates. Captain Anderson, perhaps unable to forget Colley's death, unconsciously reads from the funeral service at the Prettimans' wedding ceremony. Forced to stay in Colley's cabin, due to lack of accommodation, Talbot is unable to sleep at nights while requiring a lantern by him, constantly, to keep away thoughts of Colley. The crew, too, have a haunting memory of him as suggested by Webber's conversation with Talbot concerning Colley's cabin (50). Acting as a midshipman, with Summer's help during the sleepless hours of the night, Talbot succeeds in overcoming his fear of the dead Colley.

The voyage, signifying a passage through life, becomes a painful learning process, not only for Talbot, but for all the other passengers in the ship. While Prettiman learns to control his passionate outbursts, Mrs. Prettiman subdues her vehemence becoming a sympathetic person in the process. Young Willis, whose inexperience had caused the loss of the ship's top mast, matures into a young man after his ordeal of sitting as a watch on the yard-arm of the top mast. His growth is signified by the breaking of his voice. Talbot, too, had started the voyage as an inexperienced young man conscious of his privileges but ends it becoming wiser and maturer. As Prettiman points it out to him, 'You started your voyage with the objectivity of ignorance and are finishing it with the subjectivity of knowledge' (202-203). Elevating him from his self-absorbed state, the voyage, providing experience of love, beauty, friendship, terror, and death, becomes and important part of his life and education. With the death of his godfather, he is left to fend for himself and has got this realization:

> I should now have to *work my passage*. I should not be able to pass on a mention of the governor to my godfather, should not be able to press in high places for Charles's temporary promotion to be made permanent. No, indeed. It was no Odyssey, no paradigm, metaphor, analogue — it was the ridiculous sorrows of Edmund Talbot, whom life no longer spoiled as if he were its favoured child. (277)

The journal form, used to depict the stages in Edmund Talbot's gradual development, is extended to the utmost limit in the tripartite novel. With the progress of the journal through the three novels, Talbot evolves as a person with a growing social awareness. Written in the manner of the picaresque voyages of Defoe, Fielding, Swift, and Smollett, it invites the reader constantly to judge what he is seeing. The precise details of the life afloat is brilliantly realized through the evocation of the deck, variously cramped chambers, smell of the sand ballast, horizon, ice, cloud, wave, light, and dark. The journal, while addressed to the audience of one, Talbot's influential patron godfather, in *Rites of Passage*, is maintained for its own sake in *Close Quarters*, and is continued with the intention of publication in *Fire Down Below*. The pretence of keeping a journal is abandoned completely here. The whole narrative process corresponds to Talbot's democratization from a haughty, self-promoting Young snob to a wiser man ready to accept the socially constructed world as it is. Observing and commenting upon half truths, Talbot, as a narrator, is unreliable. Though the journal projects him as the disengaged and judging narrator, yet, whatever he registers is partial, incompletely observed, and only partly comprehensible. While revealing its writer as one incapable of grappling with reality, Colley's letter subverts all that Talbot records in *Rites of Passage.* A blend of poetry, mysticism, and nature's study, the letter reveals Colley to be a romantic. Balanced against it is Talbot's classicism. Thus the narrative technique of *Rite of Passage* comprises two points of view of the same voyage. While the stress is on the reasoning and logical faculties in *Rites of Passage,* it shifts to the emotional and the poetic in *Close Quarters.* A love of Shakespeare and the Greek poets, apparent from the beginning, influences Talbot's love for Marion Chumley while the narrative principles of dream become a device by which his increasing awareness becomes apparent. The technique of sleep and dream is successfully used in *Fire Down Below* to reveal the structuring of Talbot's new beliefs. Tempests, storms, tidal waves, fires, and oceanic turbulences are used with an intensity that makes the whole voyage almost physically palpable. Though there is a note of tragedy in *Rites of Passage*, the dominant note of the trilogy is comic. As Stephen Medcalf rightly says, 'the trilogy is a *Commedia,* it is a secular and even a comic *Commedia'.*[12]

NOTES

1. Stephen Medcalf, 'Into the Southern seas', *Times Literary Supplement,* 17th March 1989.
2 Elizabeth Longford, Wellingtion vol I, *The Years of the Sword,* (1969), 51.
3. James Baker, 'An Interview with William Golding', *Twentieth Century Literature,* Vol 28, No. 2 Summer 1982, 132.
4. *Op cit.,* 163.
5. William Golding, *The Hot Gates,* 135.
6. Mark Kinkead-Weeks and Ian Gregor, *William Golding : A Critical Study,* Faber, London, 1984, 270-271.

7. *Op. cit.,* 132.
8. *Op. cit.,* 164.
9. *Op. cit.,* 164.
10. William Golding , *Close Quarters,* 7.
11. *Op. cit.,* 165.
12. Stephen Medcalf, 'Into the Southern Seas', *Times Literary Supplement,* 17th March 1989.

7

Conclusion

The foregoing account should give a precise idea of Golding's preoccupation as a novelist. He shows isolated individuals or small groups in extreme situations in their basic conditions stripped of trappings. The settings of the novels are also remarkable for their variety.

Golding believed that 'a writer's books should be as different from each other as possible' (*A Moving Target*, 198). Although his nine novels and three novellas are very different from one another, they are not totally unrelated to each other. While revealing Golding's vision of man's nature, his tragic sense of human destiny, the novels exhibit a pattern and a technique which are intense and exclusive.

Compared with his earlier novels, termed as fables or myths, the later novels of Golding, beginning with *The Pyramid* and ending with *Fire Down Below*, come very near to resembling the social novel of contemporary life. Depicting a world of social relationships, a world we all inhabit, Golding showed increasingly a preparedness, in the later novels, to explore the nature of good and evil in the social context. Just as the first five novels reveal Golding's preoccupation with the fundamental question of 'what manner of creature is man', his later novels reveal his concern for the lack of love in modern society and its resultant effect. The epigraph of

The Pyramid is indicative of the kind of thought with which Golding occupied himself. The Miss Dawlish that we see at the end to *The Pyramid* is the product of a loveless society. Embittered with humanity, she would rather save a budgie than a child from a fire. Golding has depicted in trenchant terms man's loss of humanity under the present-day circumstances of a technological civilization. The underlying moral tone of his fiction will not fail to remind the sensitive reader of Wordsworth's concern at the increasing debasement of man as a result of his selfishness, and his wilful withdrawal from the lap of nature. Golding has depicted the plight of men and women in a loveless and class-ridden society that is ours. Lack of love and understanding has alienated people from each other, witness, for instance, the situations of Barclay and Tucker. It will not be an overstatement to say that Golding, too, like Arnold and Eliot before him, is presenting a kind of wasteland although his voice is not as pronounced.

While the earlier novels, written just after Golding's experience of World War II, are predominantly gloomy, projecting the darker side of human nature, *Darkness Visible* and the Trilogy end is a note of hope. Man may have lost his innocence, and may be living in a world pervaded by evil, yet all is not lost. By exercising one's conscious will and having faith in God, salvation can be attained. An aspiration for goodness, tenderness, compassion, and love can make him turn from selfishness to the grace of God, Golding's fiction advocates a humanism that is not based on theology or 'fringe theology' as he terms it. The elements of his belief are simple: innocence, selflessness, love, and faith in God's saving grace. This, then, indicates a note of moral affirmation in his fiction.

Golding believes that instead of being wholly absorbed by the necessities of the corporal frame, man should look for mystical wisdom. He is not just an individual existing for his own sake. His saints point out that, man, instead of worshipping his own small self, must be ready to become one with the divine will. Golding's message is that man should relate himself with the natural-spiritual order which is the only lasting one.

The state of self-revelation and spiritual condition of the protagonists can be detected through symbols or events bearing some common characteristics. Thus, in the crucial scene in *Darkness Visible* where Matty performs the mysterious rituals of going under marshy waters with the weight of chains and wheels on his chest and a lighted lamp held high over his head, in the darkness of night, he finds his true identity. The ontological questions of 'who am I' and 'what am I for' are answered here. Similarly, in *The Paper Men*, Barclay, too, encounters moments of self-revelation in a dark cathedral. He faces the god he had been worshipping in the form of a solid silver statue, with a suggestion of blue, striding forward with red flaming eyes. It is the god of the underworld.

The symbol of unclothing occurs in some of the novels either to demonstrate a character's physical and emotional needs or as a part of a ritual. In *The Pyramid* Bounce's walking unclothed through the streets of Stilbourne symbolizes the demonstration of her physical needs and her repudiation of Stilbourne's values. Pretty Flower's naked dance in public, in *The Scorpion God* is as much a part of a ritual as Colley's unclothing by the inmates of the ship in *Rites of Passage*. While Pretty Flower's dance is meant to rouse the king to copulate with her in order to prove his ability to continue as king, Colley is unclothed and dipped in the foul waters of a tarpauline as a part of a ritual observed while crossing the equator.

The dark part of man's nature had caused innumerable dangers to mankind. It is signified by the symbols of war and fire recurring in Golding's novels. The fire here possibly symbolizes the loss of lives by the saintly as a result of the evil perpetrated by men.

Associated with Golding's preoccupation with man's moral nature is his concern for the evils of the class system. His thesis is that a class-based society is the result of the lack of love among people. Oliver's obtuseness and inability to understand or be sympathetic towards Evie or Bounce is owing to his inability to love the people around him. This gives rise to his class-consciousness which, in turn, becomes a source of exploitation. But Golding has shown a cure for this 'disease' in his trilogy. He has pointed out in *Rites of Passage*, for instance, that if man can get himself rid of his self-centeredness, he will be capable of loving his fellow beings. Then the world, which is now being torn apart by wars, will be a much more habitable place.

Having portrayed the evils of the modern materialistic world in *The Pyramid. Darkness Visible. The Paper Men,* and the trilogy consisting of *Rites of Passage, Close Quarters* and *Fire Down Below,* Golding has maintained that the solution to all the problems lies not in scientific inventions and technocratic development but in re-capturing love and innocence of the Edenic world. This is, obviously, a moral reiteration wholly in agreement with the trend in modern literature. The two novellas *Clonk Clonk* and *Envoy Extraordinary* stress the necessity of recapturing primeval innocence. The tribe depicted in *Clonk Clonk* has no class demarcation and lives in relative peace and happiness. Scientific inventions, by putting greater powers in the hands of man, has somehow enabled him to kill his fellowmen with greater skill and ruthlessness. Caesar, endowed with foresightedness, in *Envoy Extraordinary* sends the inventor Phanocles to China. Though technological advancement is retarded by two thousand years, the world continues to live in relative peace. Golding suggests that the need of the hour is to control selfishness, pride, malignancy, and the urge to control and subjugate others,. He has insisted that technology and science by themselves will not provide the panacea for the ills of the modern world which, he believes, can be found in a harmonious coherence of humanism and scientific and technological progress.

While advocating selflessness and humility, Golding gives importance to the necessity of free thinking and points out the limitations of rationalism which tends to limit our views. His thesis is that without any vision, a civilization is bound to perish. The world can be saved only by a man of vision and imagination.

Along with his concern for human nature and Cosmic chaos' Golding's mind is also occupied with the role of the writer and the critic. In most of his novels there is an artist of some kind or the other. While Brocklebank is an artist, Talbot and Colley are writers in *Rites of Passage* and its sequels, Benet is a poet of some sorts. *The Paper Men* is all about a writer and a critic. In *Darkness Visible* Matty maintains a journal which reveals his spiritual development. In the earlier novels, Sammy Mountjoy paints pictures, Jocelin is an architect, and Tuami, too, is an artist. Golding believes that while a writer has to present, through his imaginative creativity, a number of view-points, as a person he should be aware of a particular moral position which could be examined from the several points of view. While the view-points of the characters may not necessarily agree with the moral position of the author, he should yet have an overview that comprehends all the other view-points. In other words, according to Golding, he would have to play the role of the omnipotent God. Though it is difficult and unpleasant, the author cannot help but accept it. Golding believes that an author primarily deals with life and the universe, and so he should be able to present a perspective, and a sense of direction. To the extent he can do so he plays as God. As a serious writer, Golding is compelled to show the true picture of humanity through his fiction. He believes that the writer's task is devoid of innocence because he invades the privacy of his reader. The characters live or perish in accordance with the writer's world view.

Golding's novels are unique not only in their theme but also in their form and technique. The novels acquire their intensity from the fact that Golding strips everything to their essentials. They achieve in finish the solidity and grace of sculpture.

Though the world painted by Golding is gloomy, yet it is not devoid of hope. Neither is there a bitter hatred of man and the world. Characters like Simon, Matty, and Nathaniel bear witness to the fact that Golding has faith in the brighter side of life too. His world view has changed gradually over the years. While the dominant note of *Lord of the Flies* is of grief, *Darkness Visible* and *Fire Down Below* carry the message of hope. Having diagnosed the moral ills of this age, Golding has always considered it his responsibility to point out, to his fellow men, through his novels, a way to redemption and salvation. He considers it to be the first and the foremost duty of a novelist, for he watches the greatest mystery and is passionately convinced of what he sees. Golding believes that beyond the transient horrors and beauties of our hell, there is a Good which is ultimate and absolute.

In can now be clearly seen that Golding belongs more to the tribe of post-war novelists than to the great tradition of the English novelists upto the time of the Victorians in respect of his subject and form. He has only an uneasy relationship with the central tradition of English fiction. For many critics, Golding is the most interesting writer to emerge after the second world war. He has abandoned the traditional method of character-study as well as plot-construction. His characters do not grow. There is only an assertion of their inherent trait through the situation of the novel. In other words, the characters are guided by what is within them, and their reaction to the world outside is limited. Golding has the credit of widening the horizon of English fiction by his unusual themes which have opened up new vistas of reality. In a sense, his subjects are rather uncommon, and difficult for the average reader to grasp. Their appeal is more to intellect than to passion. No wonder, then, that Golding has remained a writer for a select readership only. One notable trait of his novels is that they have a reflective core and at times a subtle satirical edge. He is primarily a moralist, and his gift lies in the invention of a new kind of moral fable. He, however, has expressed his desire that they be called myths rather than fables. Golding has asserted from his first novel, *Lord of the Flies,* that evil is inherent in man's soul. He has also rejected the Pelagian thesis of human nature. A close study of his earlier novels shows him as totally despairing of human nature. In this he has been viewed by some as a pessimist. But, as can be seen in his later works, he is hopeful of redemption.

The passionate convictions of the entranced seer has imparted poetic intensity to his works. Written with contained fervor, [illegible]tivity, Golding's novels leave the impression of poetry. Interspersed with passages of intense lyrical beauty, the novels become powerful with their theme of the tragic sense of human destiny. They reveal him as a visionary whose powerful imagination brings some of the fundamental concerns of human existence into sharp poetic focus. In spite of his partial inaccessibility, Golding is one of the most important forces in contemporary fiction.

Bibliography

A. Primary Sources

I. ***Novels by William Golding***

Lord of the Flies. London : Faber & Faber, 1954.

The Inheritors. London : Faber & Faber, 1955.

Pincher Martin. London : Faber & Faber, 1956.

Free Fall. London: Faber & Faber, 1959.

The Spire. London: Faber & Faber, 1964.

The Pyramid . London: Faber & Faber, 1967.

The Scorpion God. London : Faber & Faber, 1971.

Darkness Visible. London : Faber & Faber, 1979.

Rites of Passage. London : Faber & Faber, 1980.

The Paper Men. London : Faber & Faber, 1984.

Close Quarters. London : Faber & Faber, 1987.

Fire Down Below. London : Faber & Faber, 1989.

II. *Other Works by William Golding*

Poems . London : Macmillan's Contemporary Poets, 1934.

The Brass Butterfly (a play): London : Faber & Faber, 1958.

Miss Pulkinhorn. A radio play presented on the BBC April 20,

1960; Short version published in Encounter, XV (August, 1960), 27-32.

Break My Heart. A radio play presented on the BBC March 19, 1961. (Remains unpublished)

The Hot Gates (a collection of essays) London: Faber & Faber, 1965.

A Moving Target (a collection of essays) London: Faber & Faber, 1982.

An Eqyption Journal. London :Faber & Faber, 1985.

'Envoy Extraordinary', In *Sometimes, Never: Three Tales of Imagination* by William Golding, John Wyndham and Mervyn Peake. London: Eyre & Spottiswoode, 1956, 11-78. (Later published in *The Scorpion God*).

'Inside a Pyramid', *Esquire,* LXVI (December, 1966), (165-169; 286-302. Revised and Enlarged as Chapter III of *The Pyramid,* 157-217.

'On the Escarpment', *Kenyon Review* (June, 1967), 312-400. Reprinted as Chapter I of *The Pyramid,* 11-101.

III. ***Articles by William Golding***

Note: The articles which appeared in various journals and were subsequently reprinted in The *Hot Gates* and *A Moving Target* (see above) have not been mentioned here.

Contribution to 'The Writer in His Age'. *London Magazine,* May 1957, 45-46.

'Pincher Martin'. *Radio Times,* CXXXVII (March 21, 1958), 8.

'In Retreat'. *The Spectator,* CCIV (March 25, 1960), 448-49.

'Raider'. *The Spectator,* CCIV (May 20, 1960), 741.

'Man of God'. *The Spectator,* CCV (Oct. 7, 1960), 530.

'Thin Partitions'. *The Spectator,* CCVI (January 13, 1961), 49.

'Rise of Love'. *The Spectator*, CCVI (February 10, 1961), 194.

'Androids All'. *The Spectator*, CCBI (February 24, 1961), 263-64.

'All of Nothing'. *The Spectator*, CCVI (March 24, 1961), 410.

'Before the Beginning', *The Spectator*, CCVI (May 26, 1961), 768.

'It's a Long Way to Oxyrhynchus'. *The Spectator,* CCVII (July 7, 1961).

'Party of One : Thinking as a Hobby'. *Holiday,* XXX (August 1961), 8, 13

'Party of One : The Best of Luck'. *Holiday*, XXXV (May , 1964), 12,17

'The Condition of the Novel'. *New Left Review* (Jan.Feb.1965), 34,35.

'No-Nonsense Verse'. The Guardian (Feb.17, 1967), 8.

'Forword', in Jack I.Biles, *Talk: Conversation with William Golding.* New York: Harcourt, Brace & Jovanorich, 1970. ix-xiii.

'The Scum of the Sea'. *The Guardian* (Dec.9, 1972), 23.

'Langham Diary'. *The Listener* (Jan. 3, 1974), 3.

'Exile, Poverty, Homecoming: The Haunting Themes of Irish Peotry'. *Holiday* April, 1963), 10, 16-19.

'Advice to a Nervous Visitor'. *Holiday* (July, 1963), 42-43, 93-97, 125-26.

'The Best of Luck'. *Holiday* (May, 1964), 12, 14-17.

B. **Critical Works on William Golding**

Allen, Walter. *Tradition and Dream,* London: Phoenix House, 1964, 288-292.

Amis, Kingsley. *New Maps of Hell.* New York : Ballantine Books, 1960.

Anderson, David. *The Tragic Protest.* London: Sempress Ltd. 1969.

Axthelm, Peter M. *The Modern Confessional Novel.* London: Yale University Press, 1967.

Babb, Howard S. *The Novels of William Golding.* Columbia. The Ohio State University Press, 1970.

Baker, James R. *William Golding: A Critical Study.* New York: St. Martin's Press,1965.

Biles, Jack I. and Evans, Robert C (Eds.) *William Golding : Some Critical Considerations, Lexington*: The University Press of Kentucky, 1978.

Blamires, Harry. 'William Golding', *A Guide to Twentieth Century Literature in English,* Methuen, 1983.

Boyd, William. *The Novels of William Golding.* Harvester, 1988.

Buckley, J.H. *Season of the Youth: The Bildungsroman from Dickens to Golding.* Cambridge, Mass: Harvard University Press, 1974.

Burgess, Anthony. *The Novel Now: A Guide to Contemporary Fiction.* New York: W.W.Norton & Co. Inc., 1967.

Carey, John (ed). *William Golding: The Man and His Books, A Tribute.* London : Faber & Faber, 1986.

Chakoo, B. L (ed.). *William Golding Revisited.* New Delhi : Arnold Publishers, 1989.

Crompton, D.W. *A View from the Spire.* Oxford: Basil Blackwell, 1985.

Dicken-Fuller, Nicola C. *William Golding's Use of Symbolism.* Sussex: The Book Guild Ltd, 1990.

Elmen, P. *William Golding: A Critical Study,* Michigan Grands Rapids, 1967.

Gindin, James. *Postwar British Fiction: New Accents and Attitudes.* Berkley: University of California Press, 1962.

Gergor, Ian and Mark Kinkead - Weekes. *William Golding: A Critical Study*. London : Faber & Faber, 1968.

Hodson, Leighton. *William Golding*. Edinburgh : Oliver and Boyd Ltd., 1969.

Hynes, Samuel. *William Golding:* Columbian Essays on Modern Writers, 2nd ed. New York : Columbia University Press, 1968.

Josipovici. Gabriel. *The World and the Book: A Study of Modern Fiction*. Stanform, California: Stanford University Press, 1971, 236-255.

Karl, Frederick R. *The Contemporary English Novel*. Thames and Hudson London, 1964, 254-260.

Kermode, Frank. *Modern Essays*, Fontana Books, 1971, 238-60. Medcalf Stephen. *William Golding*. Harlow, 1975.

Oldsey, Bernard S., and Stanley, Weintraub. *The Art of William Golding*. New York : Harcourt, Brace & World, Inc., 1965.

Page, Norman (ed.). *William Golding Novels, 1954-67*. London: Macmillan, 1985.

Pemberton, Oliver. *William Golding*. London: Longmans Green, 1969.

Schorer, M, (ed.). *Modern British Fiction*. New York: Oxford University Press, 1961.

Subbarao, V.V. *William Golding: A Study*. New Delhi Sterling, 1987.

Tiger, Virginia, *William Golding: The Dark Fields of Discovery*. London: Calder & Boyars, 1974.

C. **Articles in journals on William Golding**

Baker, James R. 'An Interview with William Golding'. *Twentieth Century Literature* (Summer, 1982), 130-70.

—————— 'Golding's progress'. *Novel*, 7, (fall, 1973), 62-70.

Batchelor, John Calvin. 'Golding Beats the Devil'. *The Village Voice,* 5 Nov. 1979, 43, 47.

Bayley, John. A review of 'Darkness visible'. *The London Review of Books*. 25 Oct. 1979, 1, 3.

Biles, Jack I. 'A William Golding Miscellany'. *Studies in the Lity Imagination,* II. Georgia State College, 1963.

————————— 'An Interview in London with Angus Wilson'. *Studies in the Novel,* 2 (Spring 1970), 76-87.

Binyon, T.J. 'Speaking the Tarrry Language'. *The Times Literary Supplement,* 17 October 1980, 1161.

Blythe, Ronald. 'Golding's Punkish people' *The Listener*, 4 Oct. 1979, 462

Boyd, William. 'Mariner and Albatross'. *London Magazine,* 20 (Feb./March 1981), 89-94.

Bradbury, Malcolm. 'A Near Myth'. *New Statesman,* 29 Oct. 1971, 594.

Broes, Arthur T. 'The two Worlds of William Golding'. *Carnegie Series in English,* No. 7, Pittsburgh, penna, 1963.

Burgess, Anthony. 'Golding Unbuttoned'. *The Listener,* Nov. 1965, 717-18.

Butler, Christopher. 'Mysteries of Belief and Wrongdoing.' *English,* XXIX (Autumn, 1980), 271-75.

Cook, Stanley. 'Modern Authors : William Golding'. *The School Librarian,* 28 (June, 1970), 152-56.

Cox, C.B. On 'Darkness Visible'. *Critical Quarterly,* 21 (Winter 1979).

Davis, Bouglas M. 'A Conversation with Golding'. *New Republic,* CXLVIII (May 4, 1963) 28-30.

Belbaere-Garant, Jeanne. 'From the cellar to the rock " A recurrent pattern in William Golding's Novels'. *Modern Fiction Studies* XVII (1971-72), 501-12.

Dennis, Nigel. 'Smiles in the Dark'. *The New York Review of Books,* 6 Dec. 1979, 42.

Dick, Bernard F. 'The Novelist is a Displaced Person' : An interview with William Golding. *College English,* XXVI (March, 1965), 480-82.

Donoghue, Denis. 'The Ordinary Universe'. *The New York Review of Books*, 7 Dec. 1967, 9.

Feinstein Elaine. 'Loneliness is Cold'. *London Magazine* (Feb.// March 1972), 177-80.

Flower, Dena. 'Fiction Chronicle'. *The Hudson Review,* (Spring, 1981) 105-16.

Gindin, James. " 'Gimmick' and Metaphor in the Novels of William Golding". *Modern Fiction Studies,* VI (Summer 1960), 145-52. Reprinted in *Postwar British Fiction*: New Accents & Attitudes. Berkeley: University of California Press, 1962, 196-206.

Goldberg, Gerald Jay. 'The Search for the Artist in some recent Britiah Fiction'. *South Atlantic Quarterly,* LXII (Summer 1963), 387-401

Gordon, David J. 'The Scorpion God'. *Saturday Review,* 5 Feb. 1972, 72-76.

Green, Peter. 'The World of William Golding', Review of *English Literature,* 1 (April, 1960), 62-72.

Gregor, Ian and Mark Kinkead-Weeks, 'The Strange Case of Mr. Golding and His Critics', *Twentieth Century,* CLXVII (Feb 1960).

Hanlon, Kevin. 'Golding's *Darkness Visible-* The Human Condition', *The Month* (December, 1987), 473-77.

Haule, James M. 'Setting The World on Fire" Angus Wilson and the Problem of Evil', *Twentieth Century Literature* (Summer, 1992), 453-65.

Hicks, Granville. 'Cast in a Comedy of Manners: *Saturday Review*, 14 Oct. 1967. 25.

Hoagland, Edward. 'The Scorpion God' *The New York Times Book Review*, LXXVII (Feb. 6, 1972), 6.

Hynes, Samuel. 'Novels of a Religious Man'. *Commonweal*, LXXI (March 18, 1960), 673-75.

Johnston, Arnold. 'Innovation and Rediscovery in Golding's *The Pyramid*' in *Contemporary Literary Criticism*, ed. Carolyn Riley, Vol. e Michigan: Gale Research Company, 1975, 198-200.

Kermode, Frank. 'The Novels of William Golding' *International Literary Annual*, No.3 (1961), 11-29.

—————— 'The Meaning of it all'. *Books and Bookmen*, Oct. 1959, 9 – 10.

—————— 'The Case for William Golding' *The New York Review of Books*, 30 April 1964, 3-4.

—————— ' The British Novel Lives' *The Atlantic Monthly*, 230 (July, 1972), 85 – 88.

—————— ' Superplot'. *The London Review of Books*, 1 March to 14 March 1984, 15-16.

Lively, P. A review of 'Rites of Passage'. *Encounter* 56 (January 81), 53-9.

Lodge, David. 'William golding'. Spectator, 10 April, 1964, 489-90.

Malin, Irving. 'The Elements of William Golding', in *Contempopary British Novelists*, ed. Shapiro, C. Cardondale: Southern Illinois University Press, 1965, 36-47.

—————— 'Transcendental Messages'. *Virginia Quarterly Review* , 56 (Summer, 1980), 573-76.

Marcus, Steven. 'The Novel Again'. *Partisan Review*, XXIX (Spring 1962),171-195.

Martin, Seymour - Smith. 'Golding's Pyramid'. *Spectator*, 30 June 1967, 768.

May, Derwent. 'Fiery Fanaticism'. *Saturday Review*, 5 Jan 1980, 48-49.

Mc Cabe, Bernard. 'Manichaen Depressive'. *Commonweal*, 26 Sep, 1980, 534-6.

Medcalf, Stephen. 'Into the Southern Seas', *Times Literary Supplement* (March 17, 1989), 25-27.

Mitgang, Herbert. 'William Golding's World'. *New York Times Book Review*, 2 Nov. 1980, 47.

Mittleman, Leslie B. "A review of 'Darkness Visible", *World Literature Today*, 54 (Summer 1980) 432-33.

Morrison, Blake. 'In death as in life', a review of The *Paper Men* in *Times Literary Supplement* (March 2, 1984), 215-16.

Oates, Joyce Carol. 'Books and Arts: *Darkness Visible*', *The New Republic*, 8 Dec. 1979, 32-4.

Paulin, Tom. 'The Fire Monster'. *Encounter*, LIV (Jan. 1980), 57-58.

Pemberton, Oliver. *William Golding*. London: Longmans Green, 1969.

Peter, John. 'The Fables of William Golding'. *Kenyon Review*, XIX (Autumn, 1967), 577-92.

Plimpton, George. 'Without the evil to endure'. *The New York Times Book Review*, 29 July 1962, 4.

Ramkrishna, N. 'Myth and Fable in the Novels of William Golding', *Triveni* (Oct - Dec. 1982), 74-80.

Redpath, Philip. 'What the water said: plot, sub-plot and criticism in *The Paper Men* , *Critical Quarterly*, Vol. 26, no.4, 66-79.

Saraiya, Indu. 'A passage to Earth's End', *The Times of India*, (March 4, 1990), 4.

Stade, George. 'Sailing Through Symbolic Seas', *The New York Times Book Review*, 2 Nov. 1980, 7.

Stape, J. H. 'Fiction in the Wild, Modern Manner' : Metanarrative Gesture in William Golding's *To the End of the Earth* Triligy, *Twentieth Century Literature* (Summer, 1992), 226-39.

Sullivan, Walter. 'The Feckless present, the Unredeemed Past : Some Recent Novels'. *Sewanee Review,* 88 (Summer 1980), 432-41.

Taubman, Robert. 'Menat Sea' *London Review of Books* , 6 Nov. – 19 Nov. 1980, 10-11.

Towers, Robert. 'The Good Ship Britannia'. *The New York Review of Books* 18 Dec. 1980.

Tuohy, Frank. 'Baptism by Fire'. *The Times Literary Supplement,* 23 Nov. 1979, 41.

Walker, Marshall. 'William Golding : From Paradigm to Pyramid'. *Studies in the Literary Imagination,* II (Oct. 1969), 67-82.

Webb, W.L. 'Those in peril on the sea'. *The Guardian,* 26, Oct. 1980, 20.

Whitehead, John. 'A conducted tour to the Pyramid'. *London Magazine,* 7 (June 1967), 100-104.

Unsigned. 'Voyage of Discovery', *The Times of India* (June w22, 1993).

——————————. 'The Cost of a Vision'. *Times Literary Supplement,* 16 April 1964, 310.

——————————. 'Down to Earth'. *The Times Literary Supplement,* 1971, 481.

——————————. 'Origins of Species'. *The Times Literary Supplement,* 5 Nov. 1971, 1381.

Index